W9-BSM-156

Orchids

a guide to cultivation

Orchids
a guide to cultivation

Keith Marshall

The Crowood Press

First published in 2004 by
The Crowood Press Ltd
Ramsbury, Marlborough
Wiltshire SN8 2HR

www.crowood.com

British Library Cataloguing-in-Publication Data
A catalogue record for this book is available from the British Library.

ISBN 1 86126 642 1

Acknowledgements
I would like to thank Vicki, my wife, for her encouragement during the time I have spent writing this book, and for her skill in producing the illustrations.

I also extend my gratitude to Graham Yearsley and Conrad Knowles for providing many of the photographs and to members of The North of England Orchid Society for providing the plants to be photographed and to friends in the Society for their advice and companionship over the years.

Typeset by D & N Publishing
Lowesden Business Park, Hungerford, Berkshire.

Printed and bound in Singapore by Craft Print International

Contents

Introduction

Why would anyone want to grow orchids when it is said that they are difficult to grow, they look plastic, they are parasitic and they need special conditions? If this were true, why on earth would anyone want to bother with such problematic plants? But these ideas are nothing more than old wives' tales. It is my intention to put these myths to rest. I shall show you how easy orchids are to cultivate; you will discover that you do not even need a greenhouse – a window sill that has good light is more than adequate.

The botanical family Orchidaceae makes up one of the largest groups of flowering plants on earth. There are 25,000 to 30,000 species, which are divided into 750 genera and from these there are many thousands of hybrids. The first orchid to be mentioned in writing, by a Greek named Theophrastus in about 300BC, appears to be *Orchis*, a European terrestrial genus. This name was used because the plants have tuberous roots that resemble a pair of testicles – *orchis* from the Greek *orkhis* meaning testicle. The orchid languished in obscurity until the sixteenth century when, in the mid-1500s, the first tropical species reached Europe. Vanilla was mentioned in 1552 but had, in fact, come into Europe some decades earlier in the form of pods that were used for flavouring and vanilla still remains the only orchid of any commercial value. There are other orchids that are used in Oriental medicines, but have nothing like the world-wide usage of vanilla. *Disa unflora*, a species that grows in South Africa, was described in 1688, but it was from Asia that many new species arrived in Europe. In the seventeenth century exploration had become widespread, particularly in Asia, and the genus *Dendrobium* was one of the first to be described. With all these new species being collected there was much activity to describe and place all these new discoveries into botanical groups.

The early attempts at classification were hit and miss, with plants being placed in debatable genera. In 1735 Carl von Linné, the Swedish botanist, devised the system known by his name (the Linnaean) and described sixty-nine species in eight genera. This system is still used today, with all plant and animal species divided as follows:

all family names end with -aceae, as in Orchidaceae
sub-family names end with -oideae, as in Orchidoideae
tribe names end with -eae, as in Vandeae
sub-tribe names end with -inae, as in Vandinae
only genera and species names are printed in italics
genera names end with -a, -e, -as, -is, -m or -us, as in *Vanda*
the species' name ending should agree with the generic ending, as in *Vanda denisoniana*
likewise subspecies and variety name endings should agree with the species and generic ending, as in var. *herbarica*.

Hence the taxonomic relationship of *Vanda denisoniana* var. *herbarica*:

FAMILY: Orchidaceae
SUB-FAMILY: Orchidoideae
TRIBE: Vandeae
SUB-TRIBE: Vandinae
GENUS: *Vanda*
SPECIES: *denisoniana* var. *herbarica.*

The reason for this is to standardize nomenclature and to rule out ambiguity. The use of local or common names, particularly for the more commonly encountered plants, varies within a country, so the use of these names on an international basis is not recommended.

When you read a plant's or an animal's name it will usually be followed by what appears to be a sort of code or name; for example, *Vanda cristata* Lindl., the Lindl. means Lindley, but it may also be written simply as L. such an abbreviation being the name of the person who first described the plant, in this case John Lindley. This name is known as the author or the authority of the species or genus. In some cases a genus or species may be reclassified by someone else and in this case the earlier person's name will be enclosed in brackets. Furthermore, you may see a date; this is the year when the work was carried out and the plant registered. By having this information it will be possible to trace the work involving that particular plant, and a botanist can thereby examine the notes made by the author and check the reason, for instance, for placing it within a particular family.

As time passed, interest in orchids gathered pace and by the beginning of the nineteenth century an understanding of them was established. In the last 200 years orchids have gained in prominence and the scientific knowledge about them has increased immensely. Orchids came into cultivation slowly as seamen and travellers brought back species. Then, as interest quickened, plant hunters were dispatched to all parts of the world to search out new species. The royal family and the landed gentry built special glasshouses in which to establish orchid collections. In 1730 Frederick, Prince of Wales, had made on the estate he leased, the gardens which are now the Royal Botanic Gardens, Kew. In 1841 a scientific institute was established and from then on orchids were part of the collection.

In the early days it was not understood what these tropical plants needed as far as cultural requirements were concerned. Those that brought the plants back from overseas were not botanists; they may have been seamen who bought orchids from local people and later sold them for gain, or other travellers seeing some profit in these and other exotic plants. Little or only scanty information would have been available as to the conditions in the places where they grew, other than that they were tropical, hot and wet. From such information the recipients of these plants had structures built which were heated by large stoves. They had brick walls up to the eaves, with flues within the walls for the hot air to pass; they were surmounted by a solid roof and were known as 'stove houses'. As a result, they were like Turkish baths because water was liberally poured over the walls and floor to create humidity. One commentator of the time, although a lover of orchids, is said to have objected to the 'stew-pan conditions' that they had to be viewed in. It is not surprising therefore to read that not many of the plants thus housed survived.

With the coming of cast-iron structures, proper boilers and water-filled, cast-iron pipes, glasshouses as we recognize today came into being. Even so, the cooler growing orchids did not do quite as well as they should. It took some time for more reliable information to be gathered by botanists on the plants in the wild and to make drawings of them. They also carried more scientific instruments with which to take proper readings. With such information it was now possible to alter the environment within the glasshouses. Many would have been surprised to discover that not all tropical orchids needed high temperatures – they had not been to their habitats. They knew well enough that it became colder as you ascended the Alps, but they did not realize just how cool it became with altitude in the tropics. At this juncture the orchid house may well have been divided into the three temperature zones we know today – cool, intermediate and warm (hot). These zones relate to the conditions experienced in the locations where the orchids are found and in culture indicate the minimum winter temperature at which the plants will continue to grow healthily.

Since the end of the Second World War orchids have become less expensive, they are now no longer the possessions of the wealthy. Modern propagation techniques and reasonably inexpensive fuel have made them available to all. The developments in orchid culture over the last two centuries have meant that today we are easily able to grow the plants that in 1809 – the year the Horticultural Society of London, later to become the Royal Horticultural Society, was founded – were so difficult to cultivate. John Lindley, renowned today as the father of orchid culture, said, 'Orchids must be grown in conditions as near as possible to those of their natural surroundings'; this is still true, but up to a point. In our greenhouses we endeavour to maintain fairly high humidity levels and obviously

ABOVE: *The Wardian case was an advanced design used by wealthy Victorians who owned conservatories. These cases were used to house orchids and other tender plants, a sort of greenhouse within a greenhouse. The original Wardian case was a simple wood and glass box that allowed the plants being transported on the open decks of ships to be protected from the weather.*

maintain minimum temperatures; but in our homes conditions are very different, yet we can still grow orchids easily. What is significant for orchid culture since Lindley's time are the developments in composts and the discovery of basket and raft cultivation. Modern lighting and shading techniques, automatic ventilation, reliable thermostats and the zoning of the greenhouse have all helped. Advances in the understanding of how orchid seed germinates and the developments of micro-propagation have meant that orchids may now be grown without the problems of the nineteenth-century growers. This has also brought down prices. An orchid now will cost about £10, while in 1885 a *Vanda* orchid sold for £180. To put this into perspective, consider a servant who would have earned thirty shillings (£1.50) a month and compare this with today's wage of £6.50 an hour. Today's cleaner would work two hours and be able to buy an orchid, but a maid in 1880 would take five years to earn enough to buy the *Vanda*.

Detail of a Chinese door panel carved with a cymbidium.

Orchids are to be found growing everywhere today, in the office, in the home and in the greenhouse. They are grown easily on the kitchen windowsill and in special cabinets in living rooms. People adapt roof spaces and attics to accommodate them; the cellar can also be used. We shall look at orchid growing in detail throughout this book and you will discover they are not the problematic plants they once were held to be. You will also discover that a health warning should be issued with each plant – orchids are fun and interesting but addictive.

PART 1
GENERAL INFORMATION

CHAPTER 1

What Are Orchids?

We have seen how many species there are worldwide, and at first glance they all look very different from each other. Orchids are primarily divided into two types: there are the terrestrial species and the epiphytic species. The terrestrial species are those that live with their roots in the ground. They may have a tuberous root, as with *Orchis* species, or they may have rather thick roots, as with the *Paphiopedilum* species. The epiphytic species are those generally confined to the tropical or sub-tropical regions of the world and these constitute the majority of cultivated orchids. The term 'epiphyte' refers to one plant that uses another, usually a tree, for its support. The epiphytes are not parasites, as the epiphyte does not gain any nutrients from the host on which it sits.

WHAT MAKES AN ORCHID AN ORCHID?

All orchids are classed as monocotyledons. The veins of their leaves all run parallel along the leaf, as opposed to dicotyledons which have a vein system that is branched, but this does not yet tell us what makes an orchid. Take a look at the plants illustrated. The terrestrial types have leaves that come either from a stem or are sympodial in growth habit. Many of the terrestrial species die back during the winter to survive as underground tubers or bulbs during the cold weather. The other form of growth within the Orchidaceae is the epiphyte. These are found in the tropical or sub-tropical regions of the world. They live either up in the branches of trees, where they gain height so they can get more light, or in some cases they live lower down the tree, attached to the trunk or to a fallen trunk. There are also orchids that are described as being lithophytic, these are still epiphytes but they grow in the mossy covering on rocks; these plants are simply using the rock in those places where there are few trees.

In the vegetative form of the epiphyte the plant grows on a rhizome and at intervals a pseudobulb is produced. The pseudobulb is a modified stem and it is the epiphytic orchid's survival strategy for storing water. The interval between the pseudobulbs may be short thus giving the impression that the plant is a clump, or the interval may be several centimetres in length. This habit is usually horizontal, with the plant growing along a branch or up the trunk of a tree, giving the impression that it is climbing. The shape of the pseudobulbs may be characteristic of a particular species or genus. They may be ball-shaped, elongated, ovoid or flattened; they may be cane-like and a metre long, but still this does not wholly define the Orchidaceae.

So what does define an orchid? It is the flower structure, even though there may appear to be no similarity whatsoever. You can see from the illustrations (p.13) that they may not look anything like

Phalaenopsis *plant exhibiting monopodial growth. The two plants in common cultivation showing monopodial growth habit are the* Phalaenopsis *and the* Vanda. *The other epiphytic orchids show sympodial growth habit (along a surface on a rhizome).*

BELOW: Vanda *plant exhibiting monopodial growth.*

BELOW: Bulbophyllum *plant exhibiting sympodial growth.*

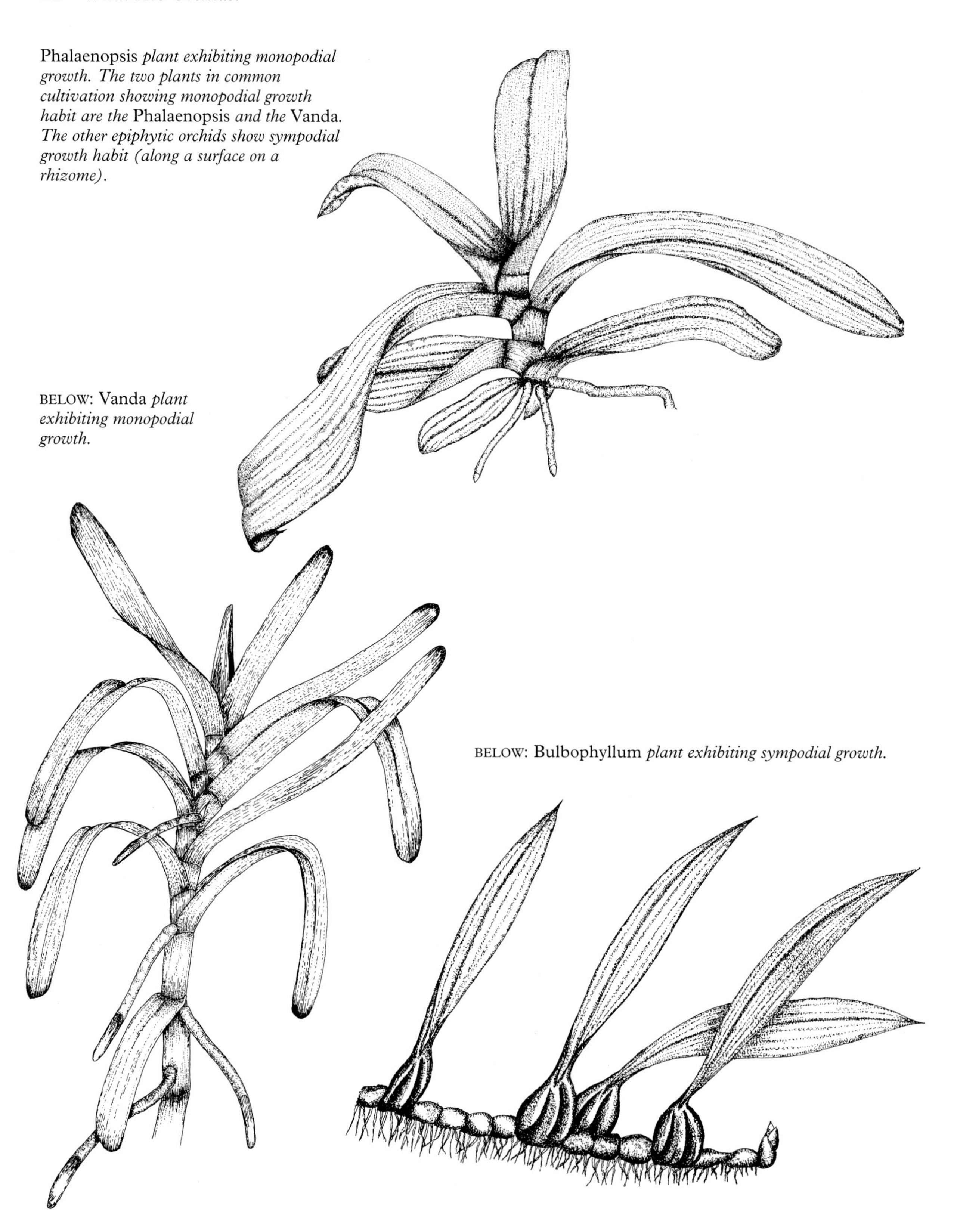

An exploded view of a Cattleya *flower. From the top: centre, upper right and left are the dorsal and lateral sepals. Lower right and left: the lateral petals. Bottom centre: the labellum or lip, a modified petal. Extending from the back of this is the petiole or flower stalk and above this is the column, which has the pollinia and stigmatic surface.*

one another, yet the structure of them is similar. The orchid flower has through evolution adapted itself in three ways: it has reduced its number of parts, it has fused those parts, and it has produced the lip or labellum. All this has to do with the orchid's method of pollination and it permits only species-specific pollination. That means that only certain insects are capable of pollinating certain orchid species. So let us look at the orchid flower, and I take the *Cattleya* as the typical flower, with its six parts:

- one dorsal sepal
- two lateral sepals
- two lateral petals
- one modified petal or labellum that is formed into the column.

You will notice that the sepals and petals are in threes, forming a *trimerous* pattern. A look at the orchid flower in more detail will reveal its structure better. Beginning at the point where the flower leaves the stem, this is the pedicel or flower stalk. All orchids have an inferior ovary, meaning below; it is found at the top of the pedicel and below the rest of the flower. The ovary differs from the rest of the pedicel in that it is ribbed, and there are three or six

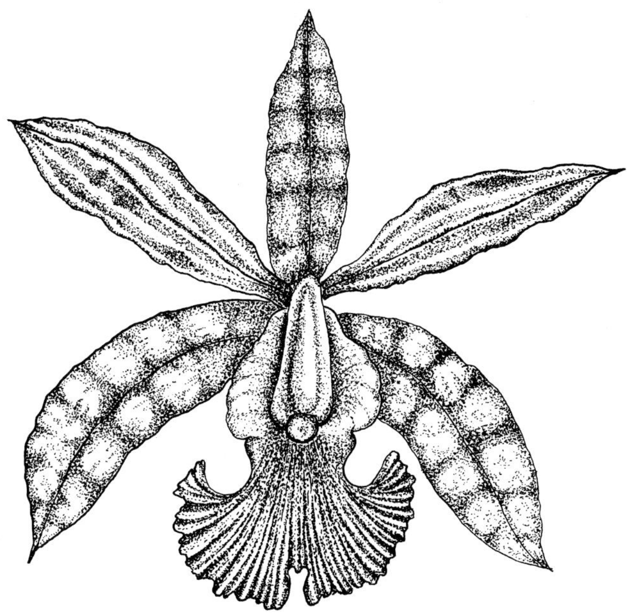

The basic form of the orchid flower is illustrated here in the Cattleya. *All orchids show this form, even though it is not always obvious. There are six parts. Top centre and lower to left and right are the sepals. To the upper left and right are the lateral petals and front and centre is the lip or labellum. The lip is the important part of the flower, comprising the column, the stigmatic surface and the pollinia, which are all dedicated to ensuring that pollination occurs.*

Section of typical flower.

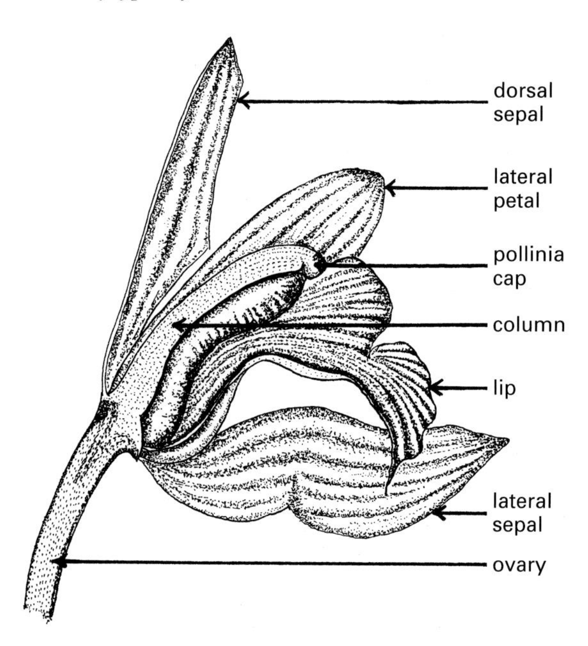

ribs on the ovary. If the flower is pollinated then the ovary will swell and become more recognizable as a seedpod.

The lower whorl of the calyx is made up of the sepals, these are usually much less colourful than the rest of the flower. They formed the outer protective covering when the flower was in bud. The next whorl is formed by the petals; two of them are similar to the sepals, but the third and most important is quite different and is called the lip or labellum. This is the highly modified part of the flower and is very distinctive. In most orchids it is larger than the other parts. The lip may have a central callus which may be hairy. Calluses are often arranged longitudinally to direct the pollinator to the source of the nectar. Here there is a spur or seccate nectary. In some species, particularly *Angraecum sesquipidale*, there is a long spur up to 30cm (12in) in length. The lip also acts as a landing pad for potential pollinators, hence it is dominant and colourful. The lip lies uppermost in the flower bud and can attain a downward position only if the flower bud turns through 180 degrees. In many species with erect inflorescences the pedicel twists through 180 degrees as the flower opens; this process is called resupination and is typical of *Cattleya* and *Laelia* flowers. There are fewer species which are non-resupinate, for instance, the European saproxylic species and some *Catasetum* species.

The upper part of the lip is the column, at the tip of which there is the anther cap and behind this the pollinia. Unlike many plants whose pollen consists of separate grains, in orchids the pollen is gathered together into a mass. The pollinia are usually in pairs and they may help in identifying the plants. They have a sticky stalk on them which attaches the pollinia to the pollinating insect. The column also bears the stigma, which is the female part of the flower.

Another distinctive feature of the orchid, particularly the tropical epiphytes, is the modified stem or pseudobulb. The development of the pseudobulb has enabled the orchid to exploit areas of extreme conditions; the epiphytes have succeeded in colonizing tree branches. This habitat is an inhospitable one and any plant that occupies it has to be able to withstand severe climatic conditions. The pseudobulb is the orchid's answer; it is a water storage organ that will enable the plant to survive long, dry periods. The new growths will begin to appear before the start of the wet season, the new roots will also have formed ready for the rains to come and, when they do, the new growths will rapidly form, swelling quickly as they absorb all the water they can get. One of the fascinations of growing orchids is the diversity of the pseudobulb. Its shapes range from long, cane-like stems to small, globe-like forms, with all manner of shapes and sizes between. In the main, the pseudobulb, although varying in size, has the same basic shape within a particular genus. Some genera, though, show a diversity within the genus. *Dendrobium* is one such: *Dendrobium nobile* has cane-like stems that may be a metre long. *D. striolatum* does not have pseudobulbs, but terete leaves, described below, which store water. *D. sophronites* is a dwarf species with stems 1.5cm (0.6in) in length. The genus *Dendrobium* is a large one, with approximately 900 species, living in a wide range of habitats so that it is no wonder that it is diverse.

The terrestrial orchids are usually confined to the cooler regions that have a distinct winter, as in Europe, North America or parts of Asia. Their root system is tuberous. Many of these species are ideal

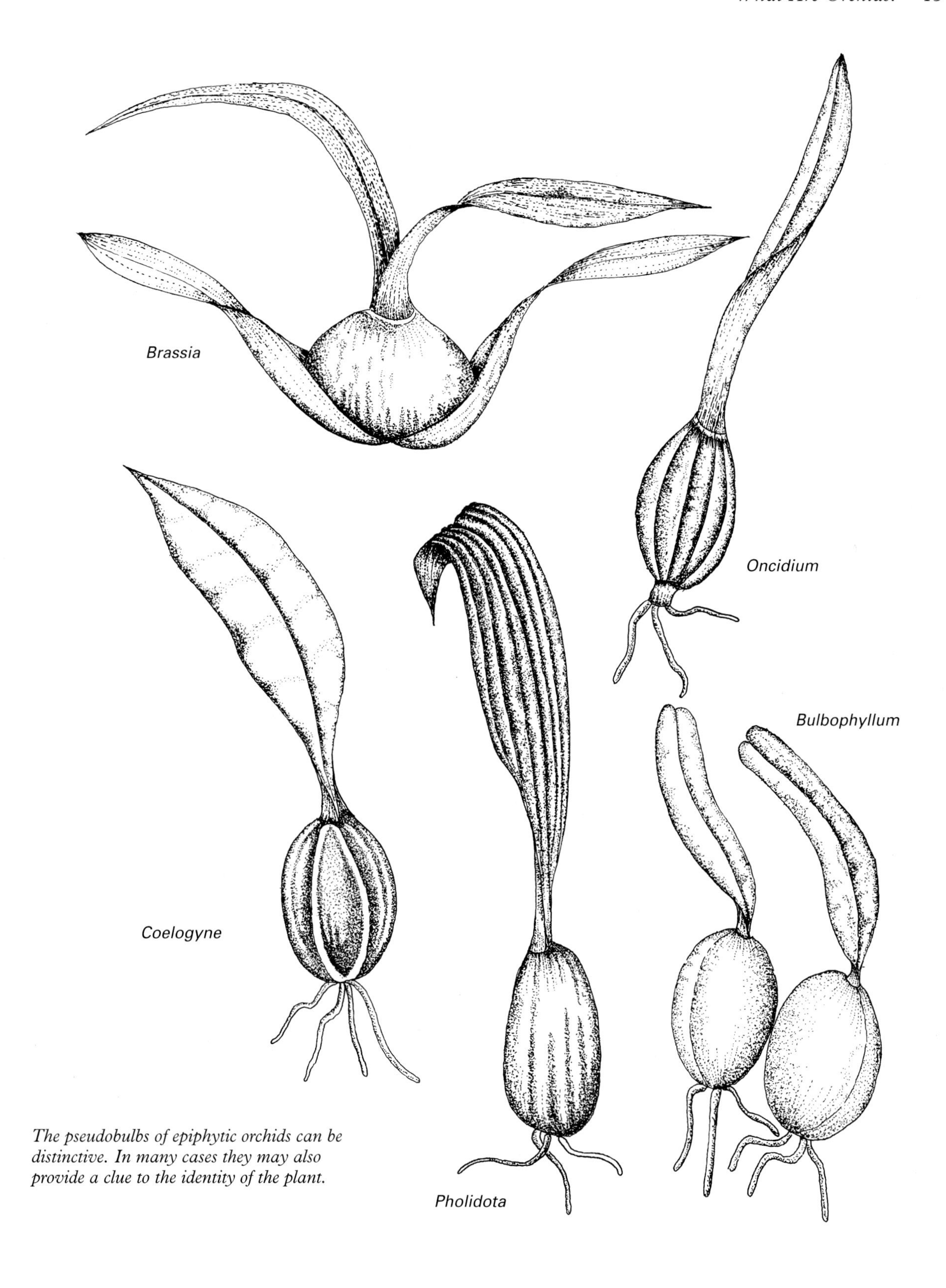

The pseudobulbs of epiphytic orchids can be distinctive. In many cases they may also provide a clue to the identity of the plant.

Some of the pseudobulb types in the genus Dendrobium.

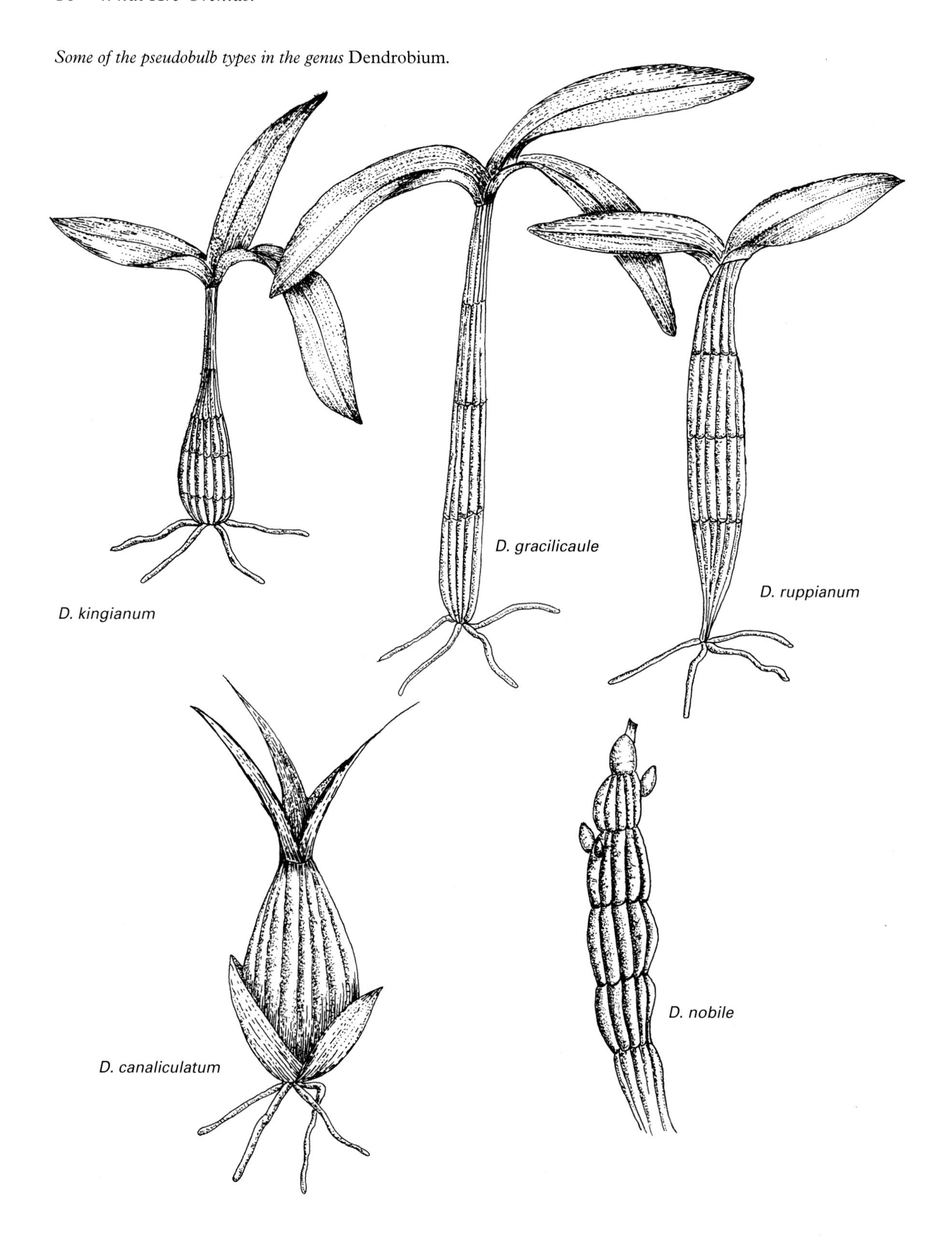

subjects for the garden or the cold greenhouse. Many alpine growers specialize in these species, and there is also a specialist Hardy Orchid Society. Some species survive by exploiting the breakdown of rotting vegetation; these are the saprophytes, with a specialized ecology and are not grown in cultivation. There is one other oddity of the orchid world that is grown in cultivation and that is a leafless species from tropical Africa, *Microcoelia guyoniana.* This species photosynthesizes through its roots, which contain chlorophyll. In fact, this is not the only leafless species, there are about twenty-six others in South Africa and Madagascar.

The leaves of the orchid are equally as diverse, but all have one common feature: the veins run parallel along the length of the leaf. The leaves may be produced annually on the new growth and the pseudobulb will be deciduous, as with some *Dendrobiums*, or they may last a number of seasons and slowly die back and be semi-deciduous. Plants such as the *Cattleya* have thick, fleshy leaves that are also very rigid. Some species have evolved a leaf form known as terete (meaning rounded in cross-section); this modification is an adaptation to preserve water because the plant does not have pseudobulbs. In this adaptation the leaf has folded and has become a single long, rounded leaf.

The final feature of the orchid that makes it different from other plants is its roots. These have become specialized to absorb moisture from the atmosphere and they also absorb nutrients from their surroundings. The terrestrial species have a rather straightforward 'normal' root system. These travel through the ground absorbing water and nutrients from between the soil particles. The epiphyte, on the other hand, lives up in the air, in a rather inhospitable environment where little water is present. The orchid has had to evolve a very different root in order that it can get all the water and nutrients it needs. The root, when exposed to the air, is a light colour – white or greyish; it will be much darker when confined to a pot – brown in colour. The outer layer of the root is a soft, spongy layer of cells and it is these that absorb water and nutrients. This outer section is called the velamen; it consists of layers of epidermal cells. At the root tip, where it is actively growing, the velamen has not yet formed and the tip is a translucent green and may be a few millimetres up to a centimetre long. As with terrestrial plants, the epiphyte's roots

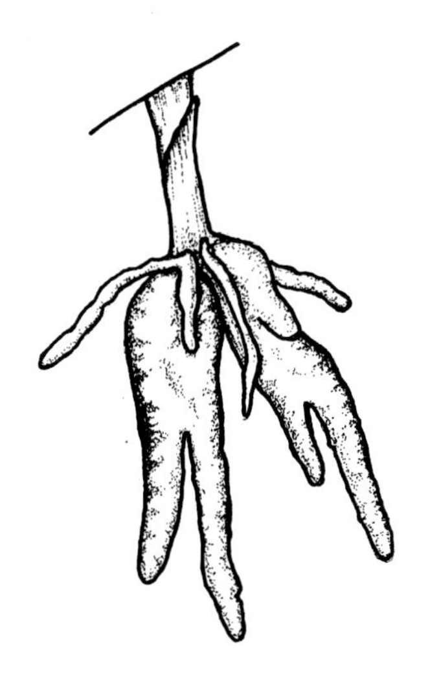

Dactylorhiza fuchsii

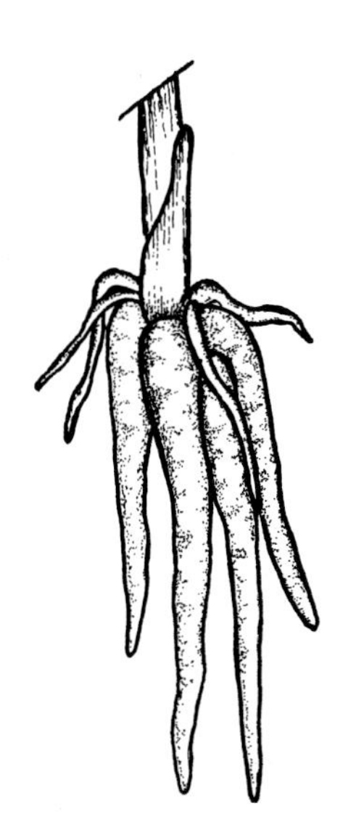

Spiranthes romanzoffiana

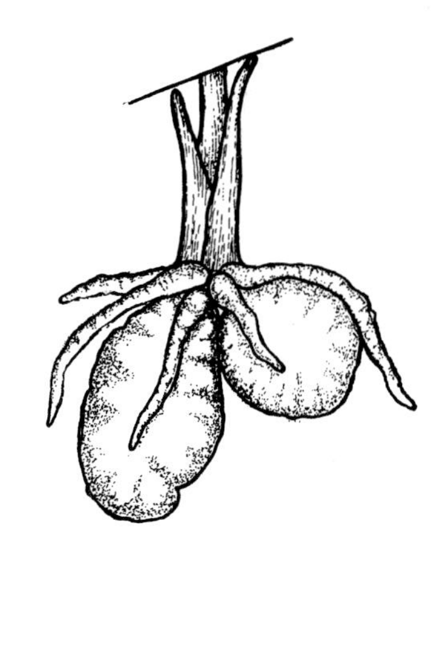

Ophrys spheeiodes

The tubers of terrestrial orchids. These underground organs store water and nutrients during the winter in northern regions, or during the dry summers of the Mediterranean region.

also act as a device to secure the plant. As the root extends along a branch it adheres to it firmly; if the plant is pulled from the branch the roots will be torn away and damaged. Many of the roots will be exposed to the air and only where they are covered by moss or debris will they have a constant supply of nutrient-poor moisture.

What has been described above defines the orchid plant, but there is probably another question on your lips and that is, what is a hybrid? Or what is the difference between a hybrid and a species? In essence, a species is a plant or animal that can breed and produce fertile offspring. One species cannot therefore breed outside its own genera. This brings us to hybrids which are crosses between one species and another, but they have to be genetically compatible. It is a strange conviction that hybrids within the animal kingdom are generally not wanted and frowned upon – a hybrid dog is a mongrel and worthless, but a pedigree dog is valuable. In the world of horticulture it is the other way round, with good crosses being sought after, if they are of the right colour and have a pleasant scent among their attributes. Plant hybrids are generally sterile, they do not have viable seed, but this does not mean that they cannot be mass-produced. These plants can be propagated by a method known as micro-propagation whereby the cells from the meristem are cultured *in vitro* to multiply and multiply in association with the right hormones, eventually growing into mature plants.

This ability of the orchid to grow in places where hardship prevails means that they will grow slowly and must also have the ability to survive long periods of dryness. In cultivation, however, we can change all that by supplying water and nutrients on a regular basis and we shall learn about this as we continue.

OPPOSITE PAGE: Orchis morio *is one of the many terrestrial species to be found in Europe. Its typical habitat is old sand dune systems, pastureland and open woodland on calcareous soils. It was once a common sight in Britain in spring, flowering alongside cowslips, but because of changes in farming practice, and probably collecting too, it is now rare.*

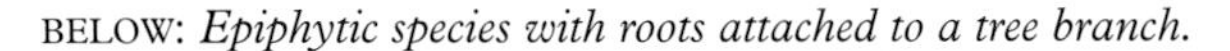

BELOW: *Epiphytic species with roots attached to a tree branch.*

CHAPTER 2

Orchids in Their Natural Environment

Most of the cultivated species and hybrids originate in the tropical regions of the world. Orchids are, however, not restricted to the tropics, they are to be found in most parts of the world – from sea level to high in the mountains up to 3,800m (12,500ft), from the tropics to northern latitudes. They are, it is fair to say, plants of every climatic environment except the frozen tundra and desert wastes. All types are to be found in cultivation, either growing in greenhouses, in the garden or in the home. It is important to understand a little of the orchid's natural habitat if one is to get the best out of them in cultivation; this also applies to hybrids, although these have been bred to withstand the vagaries of cultivation. This is because in our glasshouses, even though we try, we cannot hope fully to match the environmental conditions they encounter in the wild.

The majority of the orchids we buy are epiphytes, using a tree as a perch. Many of them live naturally in the world's forests. In order to get plenty of light they need to elevate themselves up into the high branches. The forest floor is quite dark for them, in many cases too dark for photosynthesis to take place; the canopy may be so dense that much of the light is blocked out. (However, this is not universally true, the Pleurothallidae live low-down near the forest floor in shady conditions.)

The forests where orchids grow vary greatly, the plants preferring the climates of the tropical, subtropical, warm and cool, temperate rainforests. We may think that orchids are primarily plants of the tropical forests, where it rains daily and is quite humid. This may be true in some cases but

Calcareous grassland to the rear of a sand dune system.

Cloud forest in Costa Rica. Such forest is the home for many cool-growing species.

Epiphytic plants, including orchids, growing on the branch of a tree in Costa Rica.

certainly not in all, and it is fair to say that the 'jungle', the equatorial regions of the world, have the greater diversity, but not a monopoly. Orchids are to be found not only in the monsoon forests but also in cloud forests, wet sclerophyll forests,[1] dry sclerophyll forests, savannah, woodlands and mangrove swamps.

Tree habitats are essential for many species of epiphytic plants, but these habitats are not the sole habitat for orchids. Terrestrial habitats comprise coastal lowlands, water meadows, bogs, swamps, sand dunes and grasslands. Moist rocks, sheltered cliff faces, creeks, mountain streams and the edges of waterfalls, together with littoral and *Melaleuca*

---

[1] Sclerophyll defines typical scrub but also woodland, in which the leaves of the trees and shrubs are evergreen, small, hard, thick and leathery. These adaptations allow the plants to survive the pronounced hot, dry season of the Mediterranean climate in which sclerophyllous vegetation is best developed.

(paper bark) forests are home to both epiphytes and lithophytes. It should be clear by now that it is difficult to generalize when it comes to orchid culture. Having said that, they can be grouped together depending on the temperature range that would suit their natural environment. We class them accordingly as warm, intermediate or cool, or even very cool, corresponding to the preferred range of conditions indicated earlier.

Orchids are often thought of as difficult plants to grow, but they have evolved to endure extremes of climatic conditions. The habitat types described illustrate the vast range of environments into which orchids have spread. Orchids are not the tender plants people think that they are; contrary to popular belief, they are quite tough. They have evolved to withstand some hardship. There are, however, some basic rules to follow if you are to succeed with them. It is the intention of this book to guide you through the maze of dos and don'ts. I do not want you to be put off by this because orchids are easy plants to grow. I want you to enjoy them, however you grow them, get involved with your local society and discover the world of orchids – you will be glad that you did, it is a fascinating world.

ABOVE: *Alpine meadows are a good location in which to look for terrestrial orchids, either as here at the woodland edge or in an open meadow.*

Along rivers such as this in Costa Rica, epiphytic orchids can be seen growing on the overhanging branches of trees. At lower altitudes the river provides much of the humidity.

CHAPTER 3

Orchids in the Home

The orchid is today becoming very popular as a houseplant and, because of modern propagation techniques, they have become more readily available and less expensive. Most people are attracted to buying a plant that is in flower. Many ask how long it will remain in flower and how to get it to reflower? In the houseplant market you could be restricted to those on offer in the garden centre, florist's shop or superstore, but do not be, because there are many orchid nurseries that supply by mail order. There are several genera suitable for growing in the home; these include *Phalaenopsis*, *Dendrobium*, *Cymbidium*, *Oncidium*, *Odontoglossum*,[2] *Cattleya*, *Coelogyne*, *Encyclia* and *Paphiopedilum*. These genera do not mind having their roots confined in a pot, which makes them suitable for the home environment. There are others that do not take kindly to having their roots enclosed in a pot and these are more suitable for orchid cases or greenhouse culture where humidity can be maintained at higher levels than in the living room. Some orchids grow quite large and the cymbidium is one: in a few years it could be in a 20 or 25cm (8 or 10in) pot and have leaves 45cm (18in) long, and some coelogynes have the habit of growing long rhizomes and spreading over wide areas, and others grow to an appreciable size, thus *C. asperata* has leaves 60cm (24in) long. The rest of the plants on the list are manageable and one or two of each will give you an attractive collection.

Light is important for all plants, but the question is how much? Not all orchids are sun-lovers, some like shade, so it is necessary to understand what each genus requires. Generally, all those used as houseplants need good, but not direct, sunlight. For this reason, in the northern hemisphere, a south-facing window or conservatory would get too much sun and become too hot, especially during the summer; this may suit cacti but not orchids, as they would simply be burned. Likewise, a north-facing window may be suitable during summer but in the winter would possibly be too dark and cold. That leaves us with east- and west-facing windows; in these you will get good light for most of the day throughout the year. (The question of light is considered at greater length in Chapter 6.) An east–west aspect is best for a greenhouse for the same reason. Every house is different and you want your plants to be seen and look their best, but you also want your plants to grow at their best. Therefore you need to consider the merits of your rooms and decide which is the best one to put them in. Below I have considered an average home and indicated what you should look for in its rooms.

THE LIVING ROOM

This may be just right for you but it may be wrong for some orchids. Centrally-heated homes tend to be dry and warm during the winter. The warmth may be fine, but the dryness may be a problem for orchids since they live in humid habitats. Nevertheless, these problems are easily overcome. You need to know how much warmth each genus requires. Not all need high temperatures; on the contrary, many need quite cool temperatures and this means that your living room may be too warm (*see* Appendix V

[2] *Odontoglossum* is said to be unsuitable for cultivation in the home because it demands specific conditions, but, if you can meet these, it is worth a try.

on temperature requirements). Orchids grow in four temperature zones (the first three temperatures refer to the daytime, winter, minimum temperature):

warm growers – 20°C (64°F)
intermediate growers – 15°C (59°F)
cool growers – 10°C (50°F)
very cool – frost-free or to 4°C (39°F).

I stress that these are the winter minimum temperatures, but your plants will grow better if they are kept at slightly higher than the minimum. During summer the problem is not low, but high temperatures, especially behind glass where heat builds up quickly. The ideal, maximum temperature for orchids and other plants is around 25–30°C (77–86°F). If plants are forced to endure temperatures above these for long periods they will suffer damage to the cells that photosynthesize. The plant may die if such conditions continue for long. Remember also that the space between the window and the curtain can get cold on a winter's night and certainly too cold for orchids. Bring the plants into the room or position the curtain between the plants and the window. There may not be the extremes if the window is double-glazed, but you would still need to check the temperature. Some people widen a windowsill in order to accommodate their plants. The very cool growers are generally the terrestrial species and these die down and survive as underground tubers during cold weather. They are good subjects for the alpine house or garden.

Orchids need a certain amount of humidity especially around their roots, but if they are confined in a pot the atmospheric humidity is not so crucial. However, you can group your orchids and other plants on a gravel tray and keep this wet but not flooded. As the water evaporates it will create a microclimate around the plants. Thus grouped, they will benefit in the dry atmosphere of a centrally-heated living room, especially during the winter. They will also look better.

THE KITCHEN

The kitchen is a room where people commonly spend much time and so it provides a good place to display plants. The kitchen has the conditions that orchids enjoy because it is usually more humid from the steam from cooking. Space may be limited, but if you have an open-plan kitchen/dining room then a room divider may well be a good place on which to position orchids.

THE BATHROOM

This may be found to be a good room in which to grow your orchids. The frosted glass will provide good light diffusion from strong sunlight. It would provide shade and may also reduce light levels to those suitable for cool-growing, shade-loving species. As in the kitchen, the humidity is sometimes greater than in the living room. Many find that the latter is just too dry for houseplants to thrive and therefore these rooms prove useful.

Other rooms to consider are the sun lounge/conservatory, spare bedroom, the loft and even the cellar. These rooms do carry a warning notice though and some problems will have to be overcome; let us look at them one at a time.

THE SUN LOUNGE OR CONSERVATORY

This is a room that is usually erected in full sun, sometimes unwisely because it may get extremely hot – too hot sometimes for the house occupants and certainly too hot for plants. If you can provide good ventilation and shade in order to keep the temperature down below the maximum required for plants, then these rooms will provide a good situation. They are in many cases not intended to be used all year round and therefore heating is not provided, so that they will not be useful during the winter unless secondary heating is laid on. Today these conservatories are double-glazed and, if heating is provided, they are ideal as an orchid house.

THE SPARE BEDROOM

Because it is spare, this room may prove useful, but such rooms are not always heated and not always in the best situation. Any problems can always be solved: ask yourself the questions about light and warmth we have spoken about already in this chapter.

THE CELLAR

This is another possible area in which to grow orchids, but there will be problems to be overcome of light and heat. Although the temperature will be stable it may not be warm enough for orchids. I have cellars under my house and the ambient temperature is 10°C(50°F), so this would fine for the cool growers. For any of the warmer growing plants one answer is to build a cabinet, another is to heat the whole room, or you could partition the room and heat only part of it. The heating can easily be provided by using a thermostatically-controlled, greenhouse electric heater, or the central heating system of the house could be used and extra radiators put into the cellar. The ingenious among you will be able to solve these problems easily enough, but, for the rest of us, there is a simple solution.

Set up a large plunge-bed bench as used in the greenhouse for alpines or a table on to which boxed-sides have been added. The box needs to be water-

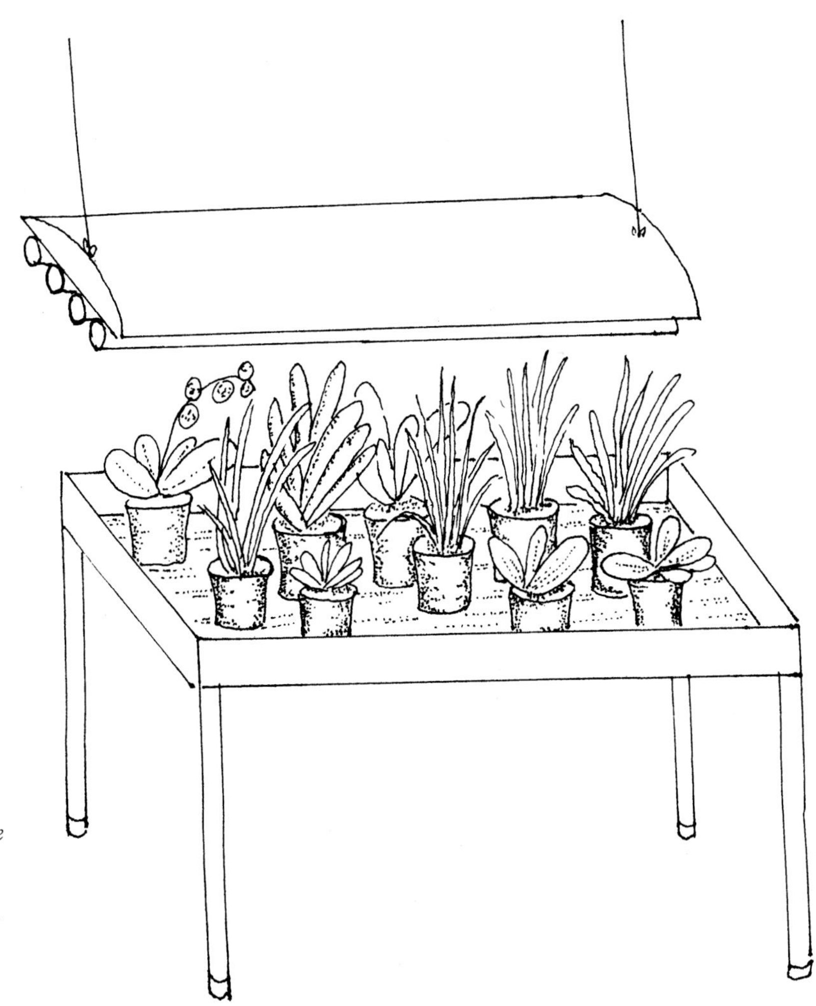

This is a simple way to grow orchids in the cellar or the spare room. It is functional, not elegant, and so it is suitable only for such rooms. The table has sides 10cm (4in) tall, lined with polythene and partially filled with gravel. The gravel should be kept wet, but not flooded, in order to maintain humidity around the plants. There is also a fan for air movement and lighting to foster growth.

proofed and can be lined with polythene to prevent water from running all over the floor. The box is half-filled with gravel or Hortag (expanded clay granules), which are lighter. Above the table you will need to install some lighting. This comprises a bank of fluorescent white-light tubes. The number of tubes used should be at least three, but more could be used, depending on the width of your table. A table 1.2m (4ft) wide is more than adequate, otherwise you would have difficulty in reaching the plants in the centre. The frame on to which the lights are fitted should be adjustable vertically (by using chains, as for pictures, for instance) so that it can be raised or lowered, depending on the height of the plants or flower spikes. Lastly an oscillating fan can be installed to aid air movement and to prevent botrytis. The gravel or Hortag within the box should be kept wet but not flooded; it may be a good measure to stand the plants on upturned saucers or pots to make sure that they do not stand in water which would cause root rot.

The plants that you grow in the cellar, kitchen, spare room, greenhouse or wherever do not have to remain in these places and be unseen by your guests. Bring them into your living room when they are in full flower so that they may be admired. You should return them to their growing place when the flowers are past their best and you can replace them with something new.

THE ORCHID SHELF

This is simply an arrangement of shelves that have lights attached to their underside and the plants positioned below. The plants usually sit on a gravel tray which helps with the humidity.

THE PLANT WINDOW

This is yet another location that may be organized in the home. If you have a window that perhaps has an unattractive view, you can, by widening the sill and erecting some shelves, provide a good growing area. The clear window glass may be exchanged for frosted that will provide some diffusion of the light. An arrangement of blinds, behind the plants and operated by a cord, could be set up to provide extra shading if necessary.

Cattleya *hybrid.*

The plant window: this is a useful way to adapt any window area for growing orchids, by fixing stout shelves with plastic trays to catch water. Frosted glass or a blind will provide shade and an opening window will provide good ventilation in summer.

CHAPTER 4

Orchids in the Greenhouse

The greenhouse must be the best place in which to grow orchids. It is ideal because, being made largely of glass, your plants will receive the maximum light available, humidity levels can be kept much higher than could be achieved in the home, and the greenhouse can usually be sited in the best position. This chapter guides you through the fundamental requirements; in Part 2 we deal with the essentials in more detail.

THE TYPES OF GREENHOUSE

There are essentially two types on the market: the aluminium and the wooden. The basic aluminium is the cheaper of the two and probably the more common because it involves less annual maintenance, whereas a wooden one will require that the wood be treated from time to time, especially if you buy a teak one. There are metal glasshouses available that are coated in a protective 'paint' but these increase the cost. Your next decision is the size and I would strongly suggest that you should buy the largest that your pocket and the available garden space will allow. The problem with a small greenhouse is that it is small. The internal environment will be almost impossible to control and it will get too hot in the summer and difficult to keep cool. You will also fill it quickly and then become dissatisfied. I would say that an 8ft by 10 ft (2.4m × 3m) model is the smallest you should consider. My first greenhouse was 16ft × 10ft (5m × 3m). If you have a tall wall (2.1m [7ft] at least) against which you could erect a lean-to greenhouse this is fine, since the wall will aid insulation, as long as the aspect is right. In the northern hemisphere a north-facing wall would be too cold in winter and would receive too little light all year. There are variations to the conventional manufactured greenhouse design and one that is good for orchid culture is the half-brick type, a traditional design. This is usually a wooden frame that sits on a brick wall about a 1m (3ft) high. The brickwork helps to retain humidity and heat. If you are contemplating building your own structure, another half-brick design to consider has the brickwork sunk into the ground and two or three steps down into the greenhouse. This type is labour-intensive to construct because of the added excavation obviously needed, but it does have the benefit of making it possible to maintain a better environment.

An amateur greenhouse sunk into the ground. Notice the older type of slatted wooden lath or bamboo strip shading housed beneath a protective covering. It would be easy to lower or to roll these up, as and when the light conditions demanded.

Large, amateur greenhouse, with bubble insulation.

THE ASPECT

The aspect or orientation of the greenhouse is an important consideration if you are to get the maximum amount of light into it. The best orientation is if the apex runs east–west; this matches the sun's apparent movement. The greenhouse should, more importantly, be sited where it can receive the most sun throughout the year, so do consider shade from the dwelling house or trees, particularly conifers. If you site it where it can receive the maximum amount of sun during the winter then your plants will benefit and heating bills will be reduced. If you position it near to the house the services will not have to be taken too far and you will not have far to walk on a cold, snowy night in order to check your precious charges. The accompanying drawing shows the ideal position of the greenhouse. Remember also that you need to have access all around the greenhouse for maintenance purposes and to permit the putting up and taking down of the shading.

SERVICES

In order to provide the greenhouse with heating, lighting and humidity control you will need to supply electricity and/or gas and water to it. It is because you will need to dig a trench to the greenhouse in order to bury these services that you should site it as close to the dwelling as possible. Be sure that safety is in your mind the whole time when you are planning the services. Ensure that all electrical work is carried out by a qualified electrician and that a residual circuit device (RCD) is fitted, just in case there should be any problems. Likewise with any gas installation – employ only registered fitters. All electrical fittings such as plugs and switches need to be made waterproof. Many of the units used to control the misters, for example, are housed in waterproof boxes. The electrical sockets, control units and switches are best positioned on a board in a dry section, perhaps adjacent to the door for easy accessibility and to keep them all together. The control board could be fitted with a splash-proof door for added protection. If, in order to keep costs down, you are going to do the hard work of digging the trench yourself, then check with the electrician, gas fitter and plumber who will be doing the connecting at either end and the required depth the services should be. There are regulations that govern these matters.

SHADING

You will need to put up shading during the summer months, and you should consider how this is going

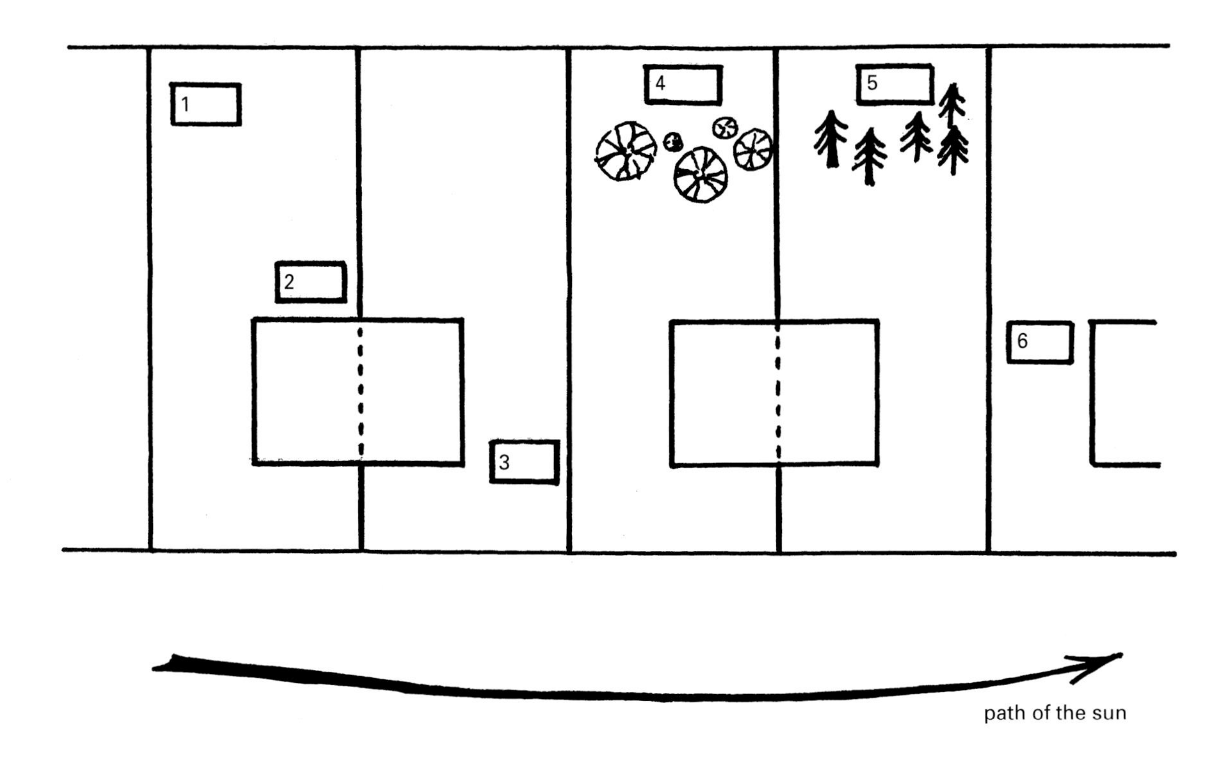

Orchids need as much light as you can provide, and in our gardens problems are created by trees and buildings. This figure shows a typical street of semi-detached houses set in their gardens, and the path of the sun:

site 1 *is good; it has an open aspect and will receive plenty of light all year round;*
site 2 *is in the shade of the house and unsuitable;*
site 3 *would be more suitable;*
site 4 *is shaded by deciduous trees, giving shade in summer but not in winter;*
site 5 *will be shaded all year round by evergreen or conifer trees, resulting in cold conditions and darkness in winter;*
site 6 *is also likely to lose the sun too quickly in the afternoon owing to the shadow of the house.*

Putting shading on the inside of an aluminium greenhouse may sound easy because there are channels in the frame to which special clips are fixed; but you must first move all the plants, which may be a daunting task. The alternative is to erect the shading outside, fixing it well above the glass, thus affording better cooling. You will need a number of upright poles, one at each corner and others along the sides; the number will depend on the length of the greenhouse. On my 8ft × 16ft greenhouse six uprights were sufficient. Position the uprights about 50cm (20in) from the walls; the height of them should be enough to allow the shading to be 30cm (12in) above the glass. Near the ridge there will not be as much clearance; if you want more then increase the height of the uprights. A wire or nylon rope may be strung from upright to upright to attach to the shading.

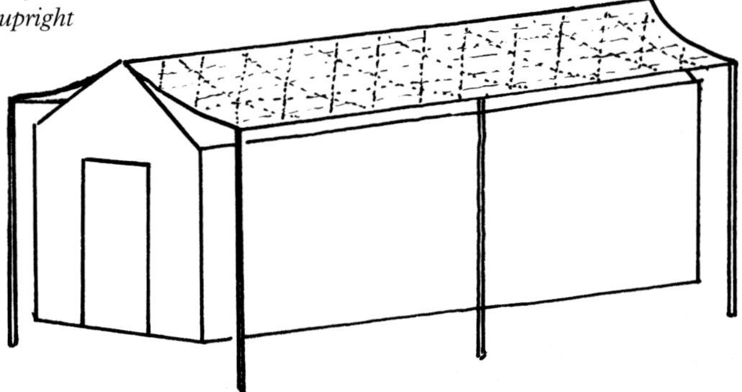

to be achieved when first siting your greenhouse by allowing sufficient access. The shading is more effective if there is a space between the glass and the shading material. It is easier to erect the shading on the outside of the greenhouse because then you will not have to move the plants. It may be necessary to erect an additional frame around the greenhouse to which the shading can be fixed. On a wooden greenhouse you can simply screw additional pieces of wood to the main structure, but obviously not with an aluminium structure.

GLAZING AND INSULATION

Obviously glass is the most common glazing and probably the cheapest too, but it is vulnerable to breakage. With glass, secondary insulation is required. A second, more modern, option is to use polycarbonate sheeting. This is available in twin- or triple-walled forms; it is expensive, but its insulating value is very good and it is ultraviolet (UV) stabilized. It also provides shade because it is slightly opaque. For the glass greenhouse the insulation material most often used is bubble polythene sheeting. Be sure that the type you buy is designed for greenhouses because this too will be UV-treated and will not deteriorate after one summer. It should also have good light transmission, give diffused light and also have large, 25mm (1in) triple-laminated cells. This material can be fitted to the inside of an aluminium house by using special fasteners or simply pinned to a wooden house. I would suggest that you fit the insulation during the summer when you can safely empty the greenhouse.

VENTILATION

Air movement is important within the orchid house for two main reasons. It helps to prevent fungal problems and it helps to keep the plants cool. There are two ways in which to create air movement. One is mechanical, with the use of an electric fan, and the other is to provide vents. The vents are placed low down in the sidewalls and in the roof and so by opening them you will create a current with cool air entering the lower vents and warm air leaving the top ones. There are arguments for and against vents in the orchid house since, unlike the common greenhouse, humidity is a prime requisite. Because humidity is essential in the orchid house the opening of roof

Pathiopedilum, *lady's slipper orchid.*

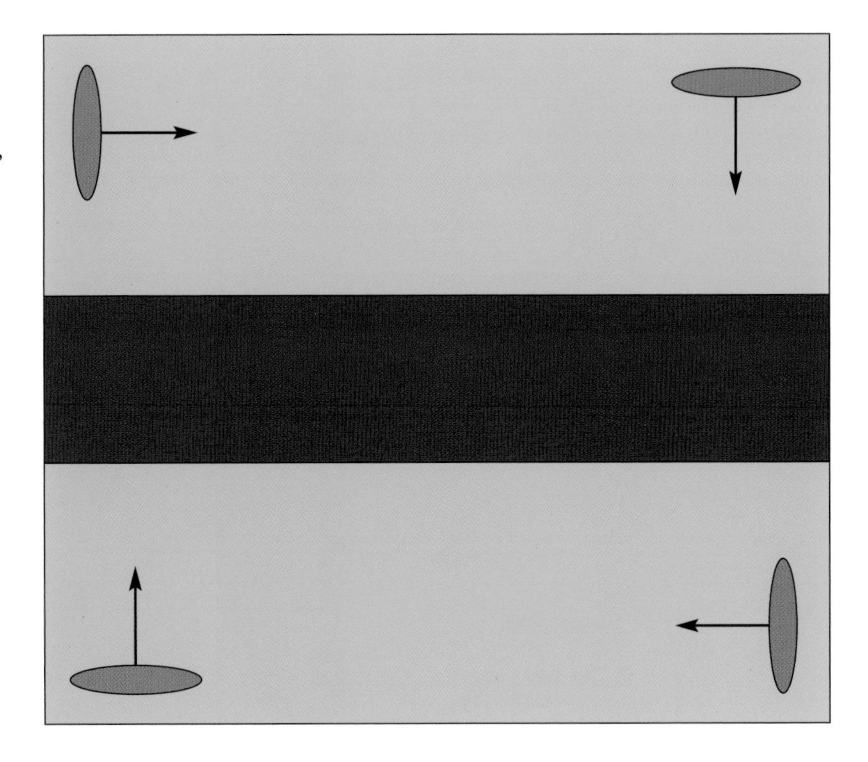

Location of fans positioned within a greenhouse to give maximum air movement. The arrows indicate the direction of airflow. Smaller fans may be positioned intermediately, possibly blowing downwards in order to remove dead spots. You could use a minimum of two oscillating fans, positioned at diametrically opposed corners to give reasonable air circulation.

vents would allow all the humid air to escape, thus reducing the relative humidity. Some suggest that, because the climate in Britain and northern Europe is humid anyway, there is no problem and vents may be safely used. In many orchid houses roof vents are not installed, but side vents are, these are placed along the lower parts of the sidewalls and are opened manually as and when required. Other growers choose not to have any vents at all and instead use oscillating fans and may also have additional shading (two layers), as I do. Installing oscillating fans provides air movement within the orchid house. I use two 30cm (12in) fans in my 20ft × 12ft (6m × 4m) house; these are running all year round and I have had to replace only one in fifteen years. More fans could be positioned, for instance, one in each corner, each facing its opposite wall, thus creating a circulation of air around the greenhouse. This kind of arrangement is necessary where botrytis problems would be harmful to plant growth, that is, for pleurothallids. Sometimes additional, smaller fans are used to move the air in dead spots. Provided that you have the headroom, ceiling fans directed downwards are beneficial.

HUMIDITY

Because most of the orchids in cultivation originate from the tropical regions, where the humidity is generally high, it is therefore important to maintain a humid atmosphere within the greenhouse. The humidity will encourage strong, healthy, aerial roots to develop; it will also mean that those plants attached to bark will flourish and produce long roots that hang in the air, as they would in the wild. The humidity will fluctuate during the course of a day; this is linked to the temperature of the air and, as long as the humidity rises again during the evening, then no harm will come to the plants. As long as the humidity does not fall below 45–50 per cent during hot days then your plants will succeed. To create humidity you have to provide water to evaporate. The warmer the weather the more water you will have to supply. There are two prime ways of introducing water into the atmosphere, one is to wet the floor physically using a hose, and the other is to install automatic misters. During the summer you may have to wet the floor quite frequently and so automation is better.

CHAPTER 5

Orchids in the Garden

Until recently the idea of growing hardy orchids in the garden was not an option simply because they were not available; now this is changing. The hardy orchids were usually grown by the alpine gardener. They would cultivate them in the alpine house where the conditions suited many of the hardy species. It is now possible to buy hardy species, there are books on the subject, and a society dedicated to them. They are still not as widely grown as the more flamboyant tropical species, but they are still worthy of a place in the garden or cold greenhouse. The plants that come under the heading 'hardy orchid' may be in truth only semi-hardy and would need to be a few degrees above freezing. There are several species and their hybrids that are suitable for the rockery, raised bed or the boggy areas around the edge of the pond, for example, the marsh orchids – *Dactylorhiza*, the helleborines – *Epipactis* or the early purple orchid – *Orchis* sp. There are others that may be available, such as the bee orchids – *Ophrys* or the lady's slipper orchid – *Cypripedium*. All these are native British plants that are still growing well in the wild, excepting the lady's slipper orchid which unfortunately has been reduced to a single wild clump because of collectors.

Ophrys *is a very recognizable orchid genus, which includes the bee orchid* O. apifera. *This species is best grown in a cold greenhouse.*

Himantoglossum, *the lizard orchid, is so named because of the 'lizard-tail' formed by the flower's lip.*

Dactylorhiza *sp. growing at the side of a country road in France.*

All that these enchanting little beauties need is a soil that is not too heavy and does not dry out during the summer. They may be grown in a raised bed, a tub or a large pot, but in this situation you need to give them more attention by watering, feeding and making sure that they do not dry out. Put them in a position where they will get plenty of light, but try to avoid the full midday sun, feed with a normal, balanced NPK mixture, but at half strength (*see* Chapter 7). Most of them flower during June or July. Because they are British natives they will set seed and spread themselves around the garden.

The half- or semi-hardy orchids that originate from southern Europe or other parts of the world may be grown in a cold, frost-free greenhouse or a cold frame. These are often known as the 'winter-green' types – mainly Mediterranean species, coming from Greece, southern France or Spain, and from other parts of the world with a similar climate. These regions do not experience any really cold weather. They may get the occasional light frost, but it does not penetrate the soil and it will have gone by early morning. These plants may be successfully grown in a cold greenhouse, but with some light heating to keep the temperature to a few

ABOVE: Dactylorhiza *sp.*

FAR LEFT: *Epipactis palustris*, marsh helleborine.

LEFT: *Gymnadenia conopsea*, fragrant orchid.

degrees above freezing, about 5°C (41°F) minimum at night, then you will be able to grow a good variety. The species include *Serapias*, *Ophrys* and some others. You do, however, need to be careful when watering them: water from the bottom and avoid the centre of the leaves or they will rot easily.

WHERE TO BUY HARDY SPECIES

These are unfortunately not generally available. Garden centres may have a Chinese species called *Bletilla*, which has pink or white flowers. A limited number of species may be available through specialist bulb merchants or alpine specialists. A wider range is available from a specialist nursery (*see* the Appendices for useful addresses). The cost of hardy species varies according to the same rules as apply with tropical species: difficulty in propagation, age of plant and availability, for instance. Obviously the more common species will be cheaper, with two-year-old plants ranging from £6 to £10 in the United Kingdom. If you are living elsewhere then the Internet is probably a good place to start your search.

Culture

Because we are talking primarily of European species, our gardens will provide good habitats for most of them, particularly our native species. They like to grow in dappled shade, where it will remain relatively moist all year. To prepare a hole for a plant, excavate one big enough to accommodate the plant and mix some well-rotted leaf mould or garden compost into the excavated soil. Be careful when you knock the plant out of the pot because you may easily damage the roots or the tubers. Place the plant and its soil from the pot into the hole and fill in with the prepared soil. Orchids have a symbiotic relationship with a mycorrhizal fungus that is essential for seed germination, and those orchids grown in pots have been inoculated with the appropriate fungus. To aid the orchid–fungus association it is recommended that light applications of fertilizer at 25 per cent strength be applied during the growing season. The use of a fishmeal or seaweed type of fertilizer is ideal when applied every fortnight. During the first year following its planting, the plant will be building itself up and may therefore be under some stress. It is a good idea therefore to mollycoddle it somewhat. Give it some shade, do not water nor spray during the heat of midday, especially in midsummer. Keep the surrounding area moist and do not allow the soil to dry otherwise you may lose the plant.

PESTS

As with any other plant in the garden, aphids will be their main problem. The use of one of the general insecticides should do the trick; there are many organic products on the market these days and in the United Kingdom those accredited to the Henry Doubleday Research Association are good.

The uprooted Dactylorhiza *plant, showing the underground structure with its roots and tuber. The tuber is compared to a British 2p piece (approximately 2.5cm (1in) in diameter). The parts above ground can grow up to 50cm (20in). In well-grown plants the flowers will cover two-thirds of the stem.*

PART 2
CULTURAL NOTES

CHAPTER 6

Light and Shade

In Part 2 we shall look in more detail at the cultural demands of orchids. We deal with those questions that crop up time and time again, such as how much water? How much light? What kind of feed should I use? Can I propagate my own orchids? We also look at what affects our plants in the way of pests and how to control them. Also explained is the process of repotting and the kind of compost to use, but first we consider light.

Light is an important component for healthy plant growth. Plants are known as *autotrophs*, which means that they manufacture via photosynthesis their own organic requirements. The amount of light a plant needs depends on its evolution, that is to say, has it evolved to live in shade or in full sun? Despite the fact that many of the orchids that we cultivate originate in the tropics, they do not all live in the full glare of the sun. Until recently, I used to say that orchids lived in the shade, but just how much shade any plant will tolerate is difficult to describe. I visited Costa Rica to see orchids in the wild and, although there was plenty of shade provided by the canopy above, sufficient light still got through.

In Britain and northern Europe we need worry only about bright light in the height of summer. We usually need to use shading, as a guide, in the period between the spring and the autumn equinox (*see* Chapter 4).

HOW MUCH LIGHT DO ORCHIDS NEED?

This is like asking how long is a piece of string, because orchids grow in such diverse habitats that they need differing intensities of light. Not all books actually tell us how much light any particular orchid species needs. Giving a plant its requirement is beneficial to its health and will determine whether or not it will produce flowers or just grow better leaves. There are web sites that give this sort of information, but you will need to search for it. In Britain and northern Europe an orchid house with 50 per cent shade cloth in place during summer is going to be fine, with the shading being removed in autumn. As long as the orchid house receives as much sun as possible for as many hours as possible all year round we can shade to reduce the severity. If it is necessary for you to know exactly how much light is entering the greenhouse you can get more precise information concerning specific species via the Internet (*see* Appendices).

Measuring Light

It is not difficult to measure light; you may use an SLR camera with a built-in light meter or a photographer's light meter, and by using a simple sum, estimate the amount of light in foot candles (*see* below).

I remember when at university being told that light was difficult to measure and the data even more so to interpret. The problem is that you only need a little cloud or slight shade and the readings from a meter will fluctuate wildly to confuse the issue. You can buy suitable light meters calibrated to record both lux and foot-candles (designations no longer used in scientific circles; light for botanical purposes, is now measured as photosynthetic active radiation [PAR] in micromoles/sq m/sec). However, when you take a measurement you should be consistent, so lux or foot-candles are fine for our purposes. The meter will record the light level, but you will need to be a little scientific: you will need to take many readings over a period on a clear, sunny day, both in winter and summer, and in different places in the greenhouse. An average of these readings will give you an idea of the light levels at all points. You will gather your own data by doing this and these can be checked against other information to indicate whether the light levels are sufficient for the species that you are growing.

The formula below is for converting camera readings into foot-candle measurements:

1. Set the camera to ASA (ISO) 100 and the shutter speed to 0.01sec.
2. Place a white card in the position of the plants and adjust the aperture to the correct setting.
3. The light falling on to the card may be calculated thus: read the f. stop, square this and multiply by 11.5 to get the result in foot candles; for example, f. stop = 11; square this (121); multiply by 11.5 (1,391.5); thus there are 1,391.5 foot-candles worth of light.

(I have not included the specific values of light for any genera as I think it better for you to do the research for the species that you decide to grow.)

Shading

During the summer you will need to provide additional shading in order to shield your plants from the sun's intensity through the glass and also to keep the greenhouse cooler. There are three ways to achieve this. The simplest is to paint the glass with a chalky, water-based paint that is readily available from garden centres. You paint it on during early summer and wash it off at the end of the season. The only drawback with this product is that it does not keep the temperature down sufficiently. The second method is to use the green, loosely-woven fabric shading, or the newer version which is a fabric that has strips of aluminium sewn on to one side. This material has two distinct sides, one white and one shiny. The latter is placed uppermost and reflects the light and heat away from the greenhouse, and the white side, facing into the greenhouse, reflects light around the interior. This aluminium shading is placed directly on to the glass. It is recommended that the green shade

ABOVE AND LEFT: *Shading erected to the interior of the greenhouse. Notice that in these commercial houses there are no plants hanging from the roof. In an amateur greenhouse there would be many plants in hanging baskets and so it would be difficult to erect shading in the summer.*

RIGHT: *Shade house in Singapore; behind the child are vandas growing in the climate where they should be, and so shading is all that is required.*

cloth should be fitted to a frame that allows a space of at least 30cm (12in) between the cloth and the glass. The reason for this is to allow air to circulate under the cloth, thus cooling this space and so keeping the greenhouse much cooler. By doing this the internal temperature of the greenhouse can be kept several degrees cooler than the outside temperature. The shade netting cloth is designed to provide 40, 50 or 70 per cent shade; the aluminium shading can be obtained in three shade levels – 50, 60 or 70 per cent, with the 50 per cent type being that most commonly used.

The third and more traditional method is one that is less used today, having been superseded by the shade cloth. This involves wooden laths, thin strips of wood that are attached to a wire with a gap of 1.3cm (½in) between each lath. The structure runs the length of the greenhouse and has to be fixed to a frame and rolled by using a pulley system. The advantage of this is that it may be rolled or unrolled, depending on the weather. This is a disadvantage of the shade cloth because it is attached to a frame and is normally installed and left up for the summer.

Light stand.

ARTIFICIAL LIGHT FOR GREENHOUSE AND INDOOR CULTURE

Not all plants need the same amount of light, some need less light than others. These are the shade-loving plants. However, all photosynthesize in the presence of light and this has to be within a certain wavelength band. Light at the blue (short) end of the spectrum, at 425 nanometres (nm) is absorbed well by chlorophyll *a* and photosynthesis proceeds. At the long (red) end of the spectrum, between 650 and 680nm, considerable absorption occurs. Therefore any lamps that are used for indoor culture must produce light that has these wavelengths. There are special grow-lights on the market for use with plants and which emit those wavelengths necessary for photosynthesis to take place. There is a choice of lighting available ranging in price from a few to a few hundred pounds.

The easiest way to arrange lighting in the home is to use a normal fluorescent light fitting and a grow light tube, available from an aquarium shop. The fitting can be screwed to the underside of one shelf and the plants sit on a gravel tray beneath. A bank of two or more lights can be arranged to give sufficient light. If there is insufficient length to fit a fluorescent tube then a mercury-blended bulb may be used; a bulb and fitting will cost about £50.00. A single lamp will be able to light an area of 1sq m (11sq ft) if it is suspended 1m above the bench or table.

Another way in which to grow orchids indoors is to install what the Americans call a 'light stand'. This is simply a free-standing set of shelves with gravel trays and fitted lights, as illustrated above. There needs to be at least 50cm (20in) between the base of the lower shelf and the lights above in order to allow enough room for the plants. These units are usually placed in the living room and will look attractive with your orchids displayed. The light is provided by using a combination of cool and warm light fluorescent tubes. This will give sufficient light within the right spectral range for your plants. You will need a bank of six × 4ft tubes to give enough light above a 65cm (25in) wide shelf. Clip-on fans may be attached to the shelves in order to create air movement.

Thunia.

How Much Light?

The plants will let you know if they are getting the wrong amount; the symptoms to look out for are:

TOO MUCH: the leaves will begin to change colour; if the leaf begins to become predominantly yellow or red this is a sign of too much light and so a move to a shadier spot is necessary or you must put up shading outside;
TOO LITTLE: in this case the leaves will become a very dark green, much darker than normal; the plant will become distressed as it begins to elongate in search of light.

It is important to know your plants and learn something about their ecology, and which plants need more light than others. As a rough guide, if the leaves are large and thin then they like more shade, but if they are thick and leathery then they will take less shade and more sun.

The species that have terete leaves, with modified leaves, circular in cross-section and resembling stems (the leaves have rolled up to conserve moisture) live in full sun; many *Vanda* and some *Dendrobium* species have these leaves.

Stanhopea.

CHAPTER 7

Water, Water Storage and Feed

I was told, when I first started to grow orchids, that the easiest way to kill them was to overwater them. I also read at that time the golden rule 'if in doubt, leave it [water] out', and this has served well over the years. Watering and how much water orchids need is a tricky point of culture; overwatering will kill them, likewise too little at the wrong time will also cause the plants to deteriorate. The basic rule is to water frequently when the plant is in active growth during the summer. At this time you may be watering every other day, and the compost will drain quickly, leaving it moist. During the summer you should not allow the compost to dry out completely since this will check growth; you should aim to water frequently and to build up large pseudobulbs. At the end of the year's growth cycle you should reduce the amount of water. This is the time, during the winter, when many plants are not growing. Some like to have a period when no water is given at all and they are allowed to remain dry for a few weeks, when growth is completed. Closely linked to watering is the quality of the compost, for, as time passes, this begins to break down. As it does so, the fine particles of organic matter that result begin to fill the spaces within the compost, and it is then that problems begin. The compost becomes ill-drained, constantly wet and anaerobic and the roots suffocate and die (*see* Chapter 13). If an automatic watering system is used then this can reduce overwatering because it can be set to operate as often as necessary. A dual system may be considered, with one working on all the mounted plants and set to spray daily and the second operating with other hanging baskets and pots, which could be set to operate less frequently.

Phragmipetalum.

WATER QUALITY

This is to some growers very important, and they consider that tap and rainwater are not of a high enough quality for orchids. The argument is that, because orchids are epiphytic, they are susceptible to high concentrations of dissolved salts. Because of this some growers prefer to have more control over what is put into the water as regards nutrient salts. Many water companies add fluoride to fight dental decay and other substances to kill bacteria to make it safe. Likewise with rainwater, one cannot be sure what it has picked up in the atmosphere, although this may

Phalaenopsis *on the show bench.*

be a problem only near industrial areas. The answer to this is to install a water purification unit called a reverse osmosis device. The membrane in this unit is designed for mains chlorinated water; it removes all solutes from tap water, including calcium which leaves white marks on leaves. If you consider using such a device, then you will need to monitor the conductivity and pH of the water (*see* Appendices) as you introduce nutrients to the purified water; hand-held meters can be purchased for the purpose. Not all orchid growers go to such extremes, but if you think your plants are worth it then to set yourself up will cost you about £275.00 (UK 2003 prices).

FEED

The choice of feed may be a little daunting when you see the range on offer at the garden centre, or you are offered special orchid feeds. Do not let this worry you, growers use all types of feed – and remember that plants cannot read. However, you should yourself read the label and consider the ingredients on the packet. Take notice of the letters NPK: these are the chemical symbols used for the elements nitrogen, phosphorus and potassium.[3] The percentage of each element present should be given. The plant uses these nutrients thus: nitrogen to provide for vegetative growth, phosphorus for root growth and potassium for flower production. During the early season, when the plant is producing leaves and forming pseudobulbs, a high percentage N is desired; this can be eased off as the season progresses, to be replaced by a high K feed in order to promote strong flower production and growth. Generally, specialist feeds always have low percentages of P. Many growers use balanced, branded plant feed all season. You should remember when applying feed to the epiphytic types that they have evolved to use only small amounts of nutrients, so the non-specialist feeds should be diluted to half strength or less and administered every week to ten days throughout the growing season. It is important not to overfeed as the build up of salts will damage roots and accelerate the decomposition of the compost. If you feed at low concentrations at every watering it is important to use plain water occasionally to flush out residual salts. Remember that an excess of salts will kill the roots of epiphytes

[3] K is derived from *kalium*, the Latin and German name for the metal, which, in turn, comes from the Arabic *qali*, meaning the ash of calcined saltwort, the original source of potash; hence potassium.

and so it is important to wash them through with plain water, with all compost types. One commercial feed is Chempak which is produced in several formulations, thus Chempak No. 2 has an NPK of 25:15:15 (high in nitrogen) and Chempak No. 4 has a NPK of 15:15:30 (high in potassium).

WATER STORAGE

This is something to be considered when building your own greenhouse. In many cases water butts are buried in the ground inside the greenhouse. Plan ahead, since they may be too large to get through the greenhouse door at a later date. Water butts are usually connected via a small pipe from the guttering of the greenhouse so that they collect rain. It is also a good idea to connect any additional butts to one another so that they all fill together. You may also need to fit some kind of filter to prevent leaves and other debris from entering the water butts. I use a plastic pan scrub pushed into the pipe where it is connected to the gutter; it does, however, need to be cleaned regularly. If you use an automated watering system then your plant feed can be placed direct into the water butts, but you will need to check the salt concentration in the water by using a conductivity meter. It is a good idea to position the water mains tap adjacent to the water butts because in dry periods you will need to top them up with mains water. By having the water butts inside the greenhouse they will attain the temperature of their surroundings. This has two benefits: the water temperature will not shock the plants (you cannot water plants with very cold water, especially in winter), and they act as heat storage vessels, absorbing the sun's energy during the day and releasing it during the night, thus supplementing the heater, a valuable asset in winter.

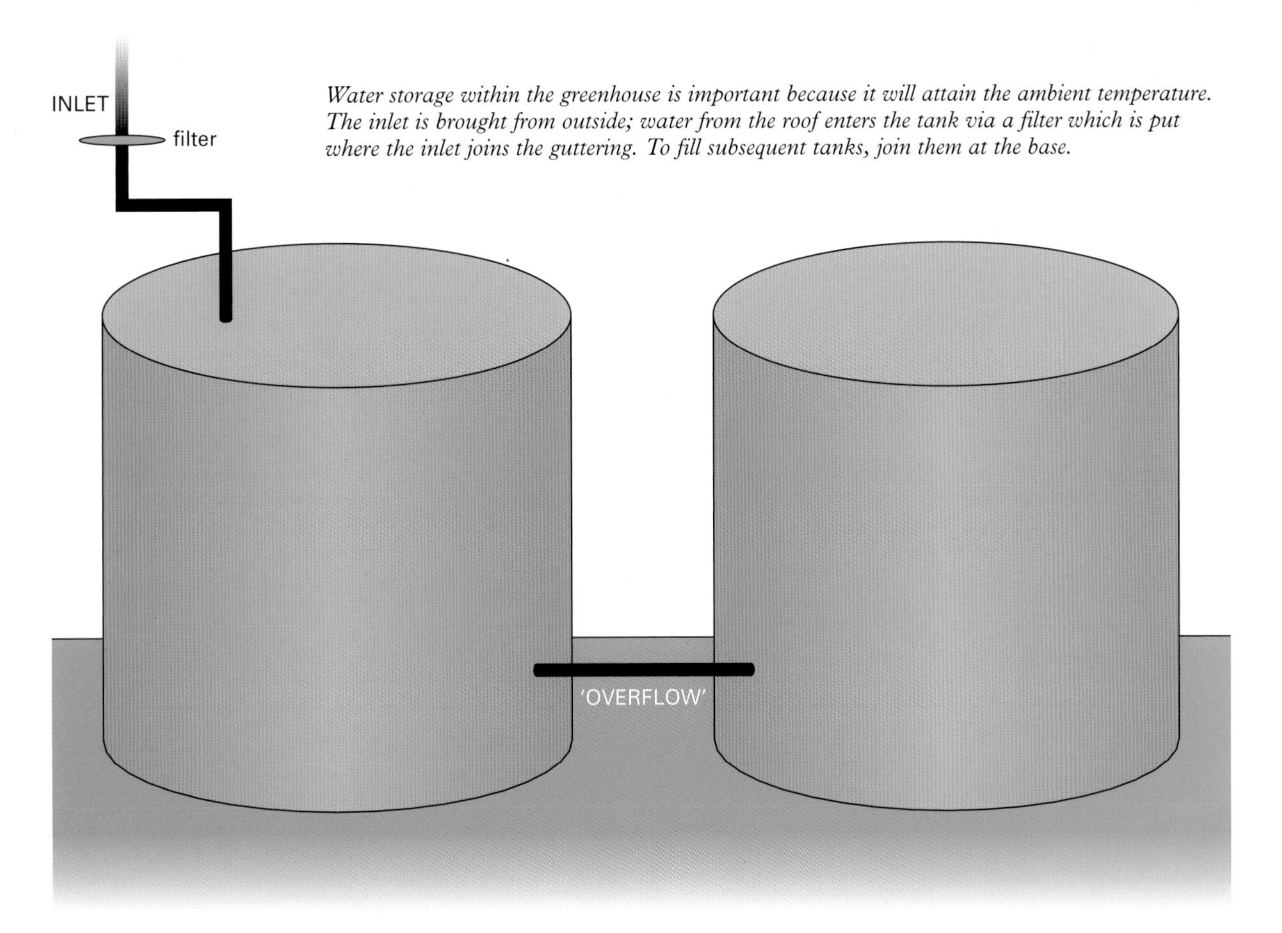

Water storage within the greenhouse is important because it will attain the ambient temperature. The inlet is brought from outside; water from the roof enters the tank via a filter which is put where the inlet joins the guttering. To fill subsequent tanks, join them at the base.

CHAPTER 8

Humidity and Ventilation

Orchids originate in regions where the relative humidity is generally high. The humidity in the greenhouse also needs to be maintained at levels around 75 per cent (*see* below), although during the course of a day it will fluctuate from somewhere around 40 at midday to nearly 100 per cent during the night.

CREATING HUMIDITY

The humidity of the air derives from the water in it and it may be added to the air in a number of ways. The simplest is to pour water over the floor and allow it to evaporate, but you need to be on hand to do this. If you are available to tend to the orchid house regularly throughout the day you can wet the floor and also spray your plants using a fine misting jet attached to a hose. But automation must be the best option because once it is installed you can almost forget it. Mist-propagation nozzles can be controlled by a leaf-sensor. This is an electrical device which can judge between wet and dry. The misters will activate when the leaf dries and shut off when it is covered by a film of water. The whole unit is usually installed to operate via a controller which opens and closes a solenoid valve. A better alternative to the leaf sensor is a humidistat that measures the relative humidity. The unit is set to 75 per cent, for instance; when the humidity falls below this the misters are operated until the level rises above the setting.

There are two types of mister nozzle on the market. One is designed for the propagation bench and will produce a coarse mist. This is usually fitted at bench level because, if fitted above the plants, it will

Coelogyna pandurata.

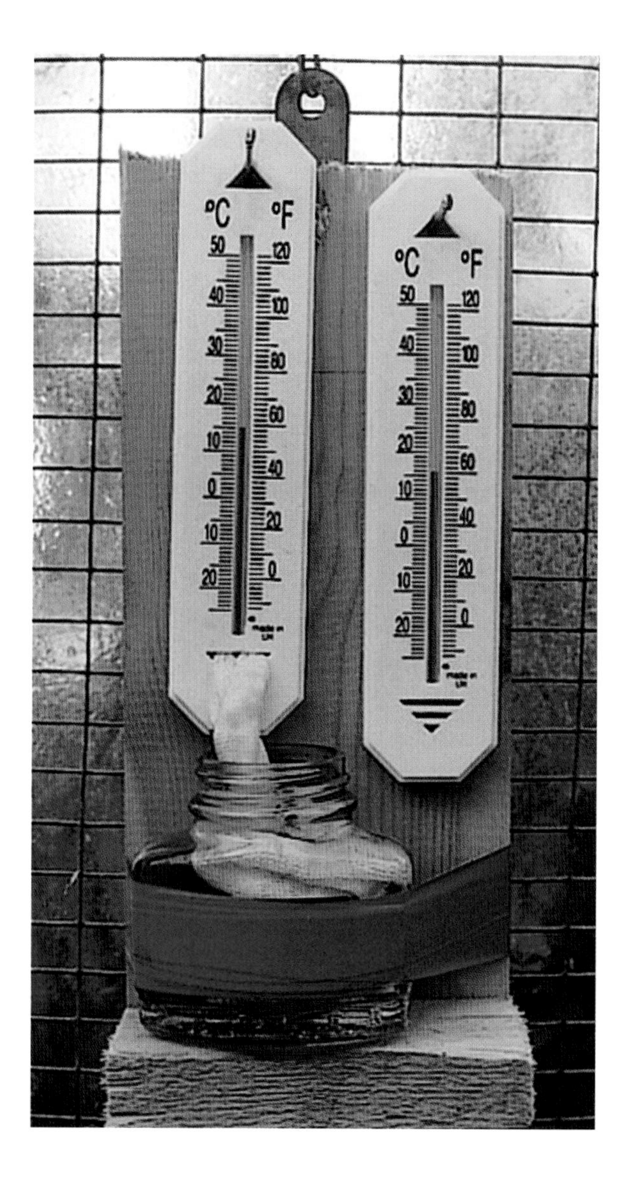

This is a simple set-up using two thermometers; one dry and one wet, by means of a 'wick'. One end of the wick is wrapped around the bowl of the thermometer, the other end is in a bath of water. To determine the relative humidity take two readings; from the picture, the dry bulb reads 16°C and the wet bulb reads 15°C, a 1°C difference, which means that the RH = 91 per cent. See *Appendix III for a humidity chart.*

wet the plants too much and cause problems with overwatering. The second type produces a much finer mist and may be installed in the roof of the orchid house, directed along the pathway. This produces a cross between a mist and a fog which hangs in the air, thus creating a more satisfactory humidity. The fine mist nozzles or plume sprays are the types fitted in connection with a humidification unit. Both are connected to the mains water supply and operate by water pressure. A third type of humidity device is a free-standing unit called a nebulizer; this produces a very fine fog. One drawback with some of these units is they have only a small reservoir of water and need constantly to be refilled. However, there are others that can be connected to the mains supply. It may be necessary to install more than one in a large orchid house. There is also the big brother of the nebulizer called the 'hydrofogger', this model converts a large volume of water per day, has to be connected to the mains water supply and is best controlled by a humidistat.

MEASURING HUMIDITY

This is very simple since hygrometers are readily available in many garden centres. They record the relative humidity, a measure of the actual amount of water vapour in the air compared with the maximum amount the air could hold at the same temperature, expressed as a percentage. A more accurate method to adopt to determine the relative humidity is to use a wet and dry hygrometer, and this you may make yourself. You will need two simple thermometers which you fasten on to a board. Below one of them attach a water reservoir. This can done by screwing a piece of wood to act as a shelf and, on this, secure an inkbottle or something similar. There is usually a plastic or wire mesh in front of the thermometer's bulb to protect it. Using a strip of absorbent cloth, thread one end through the mesh protector so that it is wrapped around the bulb; the other end goes into the reservoir which must be kept full of water at all times. When you first set it up, leave it for a short time so that the cloth can absorb water and wet the whole of the strip and the thermometer can adjust itself. You now have one wet and one dry bulb. Take readings from both thermometers. The difference between the dry bulb and the wet bulb can be read and with the chart will give the relative humidity. The chart can be found in Appendix III.

VENTILATION AND AIR MOVEMENT

These are important to orchids in the greenhouse since air movement helps to keep the plants cool and also helps to reduce incidence of botrytis and other fungal problems. The temperature may also become too hot, and this is especially significant in a greenhouse. The sun shining through glass can cause the temperature to rise quickly to be in excess of 38°C (100°F). The temperature is also linked to transpiration. As the temperature rises, the plant begins to shut down by closing its stomata (leaf pores) to conserve water. Photosynthesis ceases at temperatures above 29°C (85°F) as cells begin to break down, shown by leaf scorch. In the wild, plants will experience a good deal of air movement Those epiphytes living high off the ground will experience quite strong winds, their roots and the substrate in which they are rooted will dry much quicker than in those plants that live closer to the ground. But these plants too will still experience perceptible air movement.

In the greenhouse it is therefore even more important to ensure good air movement since, as well as keeping things cool, fungal problems are in many cases attributable to poor air circulation, and so it is necessary to have enough fans operating to create this movement. You will know if you have got it right because the leaves of your plants will be gently moving in the 'breeze'. I use conventional oscillating fans in my greenhouse to achieve good air movement. I have in my 20ft × 12ft (6m × 4m) house two 12in fans that are never switched off. They are positioned in opposite corners of the greenhouse and are placed in a situation where they do not get sprayed with water. Other growers use more fans, having one fan placed in each corner of the greenhouse, facing towards the opposite corner. With this arrangement there is circulation of air all around the greenhouse; there are additional, smaller fans directed to move the air to those places missed by the larger fans. It is possible to obtain fans to direct the air current along the length of the bench over the plant tops. These are fitted within stainless steel cylinders and are suspended by chains from the greenhouse roof above the plants. More than one fan may be necessary, one above each bench, thus creating some circulation around the greenhouse (*see* also Chapter 4).

You will read elsewhere the phrase 'buoyant atmosphere'. What is meant by this is an atmosphere that is humid but with plenty of air movement and within the correct temperature range. With experience, when you enter the greenhouse you can detect a characteristic smell, difficult to describe, but it is a clean scent of plants; there should be no hint of a mushroom-like odour since this will indicate that unwanted fungus or mould is growing somewhere.

Pholidota imbricata.

CHAPTER 9

Warmth and Temperature Control

It will be obvious by now that, in order to grow orchids, you will have to grow them in a heated environment because those commonly in cultivation come from tropical regions. If you grow your plants in the home then you should not have any problems as far as warmth is concerned. If, on the other hand, you grow them in a greenhouse then you will need to provide some heating.

TYPES OF HEATER

There are essentially two forms of heater available to the orchid grower, one using electricity, the other gas, either natural (mains gas) or butane (bottled). There is a wide choice of heaters and, depending on the size of your orchid house and the output you need from the heater, the choice is really down to you. Traditionally a boiler and hot water pipes were used to heat greenhouses. The hot water pipes were cast iron and these gave a gentle warmth throughout the greenhouse. The modern equivalent to this would be to install a central heating system in the greenhouse; this is especially good for the larger, sectioned house where the radiators can be individually controlled by a thermostatic valve. But for the more modest greenhouse small, individual heaters are needed.

ELECTRICAL HEATERS

These are simply fan heaters that have been specially constructed to cope with the generally damp conditions of the greenhouse. The fan and heating element (in one design) are housed in a stainless steel cylinder. Siting is normally at floor level so that the warm air rises. A 3kW, thermostatically controlled heater will cope with a 12ft × 10ft (3.7m × 3m) greenhouse. The catalogues suggest that a 3kW heater will keep a properly insulated greenhouse frost-free when the external temperature is as low as –7°C (19°F). With the help of additional circulation fans, you should be able to achieve an even temperature throughout. Even so, there will be temperature variations in the greenhouse; it will always be cooler down at floor level. When you get to know the vagaries of your own greenhouse you will be able to position plants to their best advantage – cool growers low down and intermediate/warm growers higher up. As insurance you may want to provide yourself with an additional heater just in case the temperature falls to very low levels or the primary heater fails.

GAS HEATERS

These are made to give an equivalent output to electric heaters of up to 3kW. There are small, free-standing heaters that vent straight into the greenhouse, whereas the larger ones need a flue and a vent into the atmosphere. The types with a flue are better for an orchid house because there are always unburned gases present and these can cause problems, and particularly with orchids. In a normal greenhouse with other terrestrial plants these small amounts of such gases (such as carbon dioxide and ethane) do not affect them, but they can cause bud drop problems in many orchids. I have a large 3kW gas heater in my 20ft × 12ft orchid house that has a flue. I have had no problems and it has been in use for several years.

Gas is cheaper than electricity, but, in reality, both will cost you a significant sum over the years so you need to make every effort to conserve and control the heat. The easiest way to control any heater is to fit an electronic thermostat. They are relatively

inexpensive and will save money over the years. They have a remote sensor and can be controlled to within 1°C. There are also more elaborate thermostats that can be controlled to give a variation between the night and the day temperature. In their natural habitat orchids experience a diurnal (daily) fluctuation in temperature. The temperature is always cooler at night and with the more sophisticated models you can control that variation. The drop in temperature is also important for the initiation of flowering in many species. Pleurothallidae, for instance, need a rise and fall of 10°C (50°F) in order to keep them healthy and induce flowering.

The question of whether to use gas or electricity is in many cases a personal choice. The table below sets out the choices.

PROS	CONS
Gas is cheaper	Electricity is expensive
There are no problems with fumes from electricity	You need an extra service for gas
Both can be thermostatically controlled	Gas heaters need a flue
You have no power cuts with gas	Electric heater can dry the air too much
Gas heaters put carbon dioxide into the atmosphere which aids plant metabolism	Ill-maintained gas heaters could cause problems with bud drop in orchids
	Gas heaters need a good supply of oxygen; some ventilation will be necessary
	Gas heaters should receive an annual service

CHAPTER 10

Propagation

There are two ways in which to propagate orchids: from seed and by division of the plant. To propagate from seed in the home is not entirely straightforward and special considerations have to be attended to. Orchids in the wild have a symbiotic association with a particular type of fungus called mycorrhiza. The seed of the orchid is very small; a single pod will contain millions of them. The orchid's seed, unlike that of a 'normal' plant, has no food reserves that will give it the energy to grow to a size whereby it could photosynthesize food itself. The mycorrhiza produces, as a by-product of its metabolism, certain sugars that the germinating orchid seed can use as a food source. All orchids grow with a particular mycorrhiza and if the seeds, when released from the pod, do not fall where this fungus is then germination will fail.

GERMINATION

Since the early days of orchid cultivation people have tried to germinate seed but, because of the lack of knowledge of the mycorrhiza, this usually failed. Some success was achieved when the seed was sprinkled around the parent plant, presumably a suitable mycorrhiza was present in the compost; this can be tried, but it is hit and miss. The modern

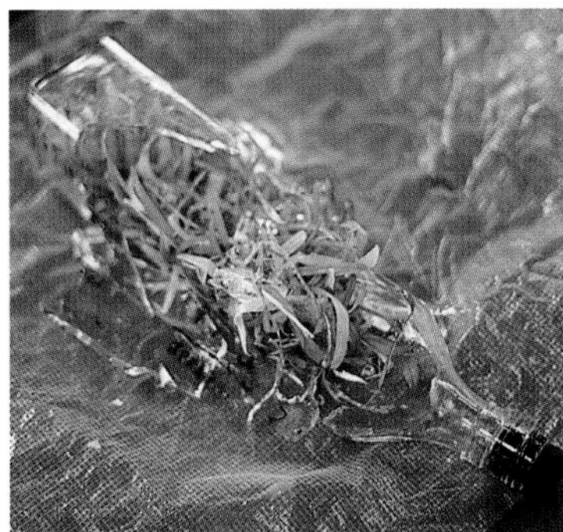

The propagation of orchids from seed is carried out in vitro. *The picture (left) shows a flask of orchid seedlings; the flasks are not airtight, the stopper has tiny holes in it but these are covered or blocked with cotton wool to prevent spores from getting in; the conical flask has been superseded by wide-necked jars with screw tops that allow the plants to be removed easily without breaking the flask (middle pic). The picture (above right) shows orchid seedlings two stages on from the flask; in the first the seedlings would be planted in a community tray close together to help with the retention of humidity around them as they acclimatize to their new environment; as they grow they are replanted as shown. The compost in which they are planted is either perlite, as shown, or a small-grade bark mixture.*

technique used to propagate seed is known as *in vitro*, which means literally 'in glass', because the seed is germinated in glass jars or flasks. The problem of the mycorrhiza has been solved with the development of substitute hormones which are dissolved in a gel. The gel is set on to the bottom of a flask and the seed sown on to the gel. The flask is sealed and placed in a temperature- and light-controlled room and left to germinate. It is a simple process, but it has to be carried out in sterile conditions because if a single fungal spore got into a flask it would grow more rapidly than the orchid seed, resulting in failure in that flask. The sowing process is carried out in a special cabinet known as a laminair-flow cabinet. This has a special filtration system to scrub the air of all spores. The front of the cabinet has a glass panel that fills two-thirds of the front. This leaves sufficient space at bench level to gain access to work. The air pump provides a positive pressure inside the cabinet, which means that there is a gentle current of air into the operator's face so that nothing can get into the cabinet from the air outside. If you are interested to learn more of this technique in order to try growing or hybridizing your own plants I would recommend *Orchids from Seed* by P.A. Thompson and published by the Royal Botanic Gardens, Kew. (The commercial propagation of orchids does not rely on seed production. Commercial orchids are produced by a process known as micropropagation, by which the cells from the growing tip are used to produce clones of the plant.)

METHODS OF PROPAGATION

There are three ways by which you can propagate your own plants. The easiest is by *division*, or you

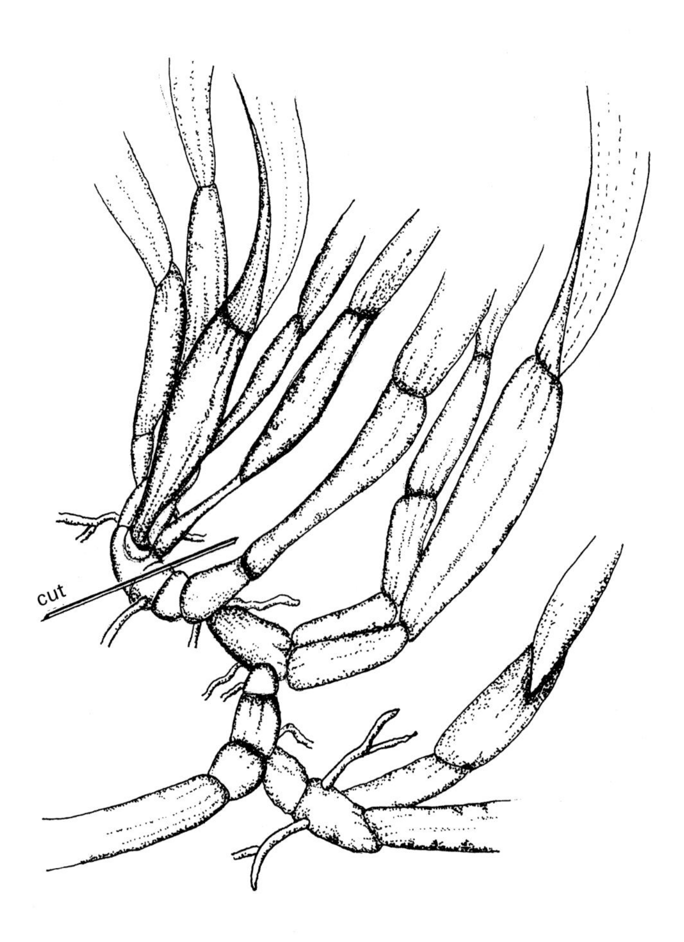

Dividing a cattleya is a simple task because you can easily see where to make your cut. You need to make sure that each division is not too small. Cut through the rhizome, as shown, with secateurs. Clean off any dead roots and repot with your normal compost.

may be able to get *back-bulbs* to sprout and grow these on, or by growing on young plantlets, known as *keikis*. When you are repotting your plants you may decide that they are too big to handle and then you can decide whether or not to split them.

Division

The orchid grows on a rhizome, an overground stem; the distance on the rhizome between the pseudobulbs varies from genus to genus or species to species. Cattleyas usually have a few centimetres between 'bulbs', on the other hand, cymbidiums have very short rhizomes that give the impression of a clump. It is important to remember when dividing your plants not to make the divisions too small. Any division should have at least four pseudobulbs. The reason for not making a division too small is that you will put the plant back too much. It will take time to build itself up again to flowering size. The larger the division, the less shock to the plant and it should reflower the following season. The process of division is simple enough and is carried out by using a stout knife or secateurs to sever the rhizome, as you would do with herbaceous pants in the garden. Cymbidiums may be rather difficult to handle because of the closeness of the pseudobulbs, but you should be able to follow a path when the excess of compost has been removed during the repotting process, which is the best time to carry out division.

Back-bulbs

This method involves propagation from the leafless back-bulbs that are removed when re-potting and cleaning up your plants. *Cymbidium*, *Coelogyne*, *Dendrobium* and *Cattleya* are all candidates for this process. The *Cymbidium* and *Coelogyne* 'bulbs' are placed on the surface of some damp compost in a pot and covered by a plastic bag to retain humidity. Place the pot in a light but shady place and wait, because it may take some months for anything to happen. The dendrobiums that are cane producers can have their leafless canes cut into sections with about three or four nodes to each. These are then laid on to a bed of damp sphagnum moss in a tray, covered with a plastic bag and then treated as for back-bulbs. When you look at your cattleyas you will notice that they tend to grow forward, leaving several bulbs at the back of the plant that are leafless. These leafless bulbs may be used to regenerate the plant. On a good, large, healthy plant you can, with secateurs, sever the rhizome thus producing two plants, but leave it in the pot undisturbed. There are adventitious buds at the base of each pseudobulb that may develop into new growths. If successful, at the next repotting session the two plants may be repotted separately. On a smaller plant you can remove the rear two or three leafless bulbs and treat them as for cymbidiums.

KEIKIS

Dendrobiums and some *Phalaenopsis* species may produce plantlets themselves and these may be removed and potted on in order to grow into new plants. The *Dendrobiums*, particularly *nobile* and *kingianum*, will produce many plantlets or keikis without much trouble. It is said that should your *Dendrobiums* produce too many keikis then it is a product of poor culture. The keikis are produced by the plant instead of flowers and are formed from the same bud as the flower; but if the plant is watered too early before the flower is fully formed it will turn into leaves. The plant will be a 'happy' plant and will grow vegetatively. In the wild, where it will encounter some hardship, it will produce flowers in order that it can be pollinated to produce seed and further the species. In cultivation it is generally mollycoddled and grows successfully. But if it suffers no hardship it will not flower. What you need to do is to withhold the water, place it in full sun for several weeks and do not water again until the flower bud is well developed or even open. It is better not to begin watering until the new season's growth is well developed and the new roots are forming and searching for water; this is what happens in the wild and needs to be simulated by the grower in order to succeed with orchids.

Plant hygiene is an important aspect of culture, especially when you are dividing or repotting plants. Everything you use, tools, pots, work area and your hands, should be clean. Use Physan to sterilize everything.

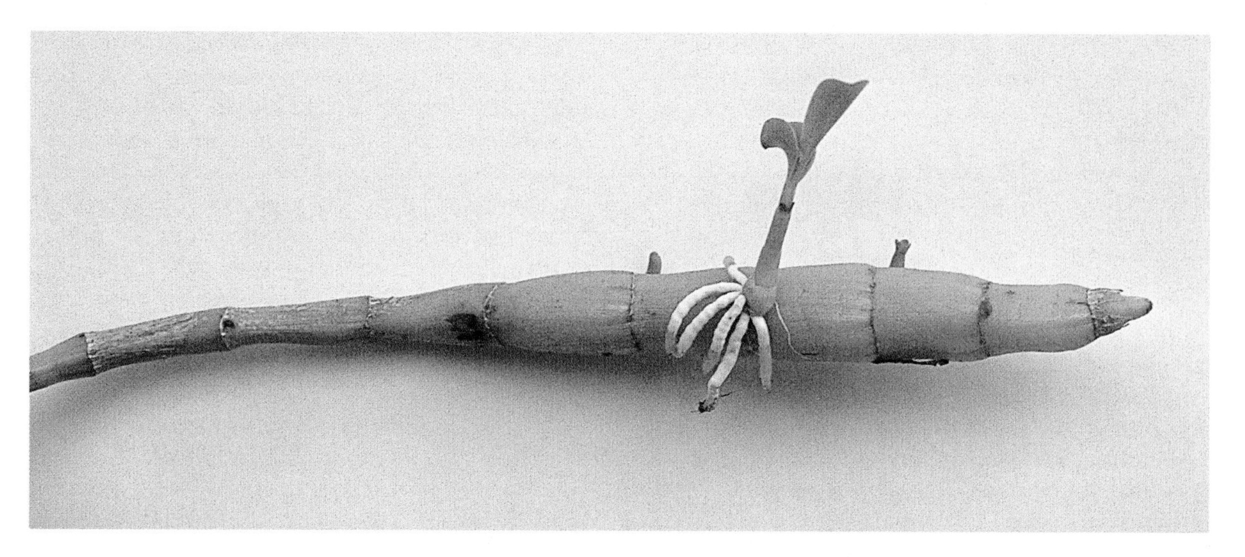

ABOVE: Dendrobium *keikis from adventitious buds.* Dendrobium*s are the orchids that most frequently produce keikis or plantlets; some* Phalaenopsis *produce plantlets from the nodes of the flower stem, but nothing like* Dendrobiums. *The plantlets are produced at the nodes along the pseudobulb. The buds should be flowers, but generally, if water is introduced too early, they change into plantlets. This is a good way to bulk up your plants. If you notice that a* Dendrobium *cane is developing plantlets you can leave it alone and allow them to develop on the parent plant and remove them at a later stage. Alternatively, you can remove a cane when repotting and lay it on a bed of moss. New plantlets may form from a node and root into the moss. When they are large enough, the plantlets can be removed and potted up to grow on as individual plants.*

LEFT: *A closer look at cymbidiums: this plant has two years' growth from being a back-bulb. Notice the size of the leafless back-bulb. You are endeavouring to build up subsequent bulbs to the same size or bigger. This will be achieved by regular watering and feeding throughout the summer and careful watering during the winter, when it should not be allowed to dry out for long periods. If the plant is allowed to dry out for too long in the winter it will use up its reserves in the pseudobulbs. These will shrivel and you may not be able to get them to swell again. In cultivation you should try to keep the bulbs healthy and plump all the time because the plant will then have the energy to produce many flower spikes.*

RIGHT: *The cymbidium back-bulbs are the older pseudobulbs. The picture shows them on the plant, the first three from the left. They should be good and plump, although very old ones will have shrivelled away naturally as the reserves are spent. Healthy, plump ones may be used in propagation.*

BELOW: *Here the bulbs on the left are too far gone and may be consigned to the compost heap; the others may sprout. The one on the right is rather shrivelled; ideally, it should be plumper. The one in the centre is fine and should make good propagation material. They can be potted in damp compost and put in a cool, shady place; spray lightly on a regular basis and keep the compost just moist. It may take some time for new growth to appear, so be patient.*

CHAPTER 11

Pests, Diseases, Plant Hygiene and Other Problems

Orchids, as with other plants, are no strangers to pests and in our nice, warm, humid glasshouses the 'bugs' will proliferate if you are not vigilant. If you are like me, then you will want to buy every plant you see when you visit a show or a nursery, but I should warn you that overcrowding in the greenhouse is a forerunner of any pest outbreak. We all have many plants and they are in close proximity with each other, and so it is easy for pests to travel from plant to plant. We all like to look at our plants and therefore it should be no hardship for you to pick them up and inspect them – not only to see how they are growing or whether they are producing flower spikes, but also to see what wildlife may be making its home on them. If you do inspect your plants on a regular basis then most outbreaks can be spotted early and an individual plant treated and replaced on the bench. But if you cannot do so regularly for whatever reason (you are at work, your weekends are taken up with your family), it is difficult to check a hundred plants or more individually. In these situations it is a good idea to section your benches and to inspect each section thoroughly on a rotational basis over a few weeks. At least in this way you will not be surprised by an outbreak and you can treat the plants accordingly.

PESTS YOU MAY ENCOUNTER

There are not many pests that will attack your orchids that you will not already know and they may be treated by using any commercial insecticide.

Greenfly and Other Aphids

These are probably the most common of the insect pests, with mouthparts that are designed to suck the sap from plants. The order also includes whitefly, scale insects and mealy bugs. They can grow quickly into seriously large populations because they reproduce via a process known as parthenogenesis, which means that they do not need to mate in order to produce their live young. In the orchid house they tend to group themselves on the softer parts of plants, such as the flower buds or the new growths. Many mature orchids have too thick and hard an epidermis for the mouthparts of the aphid to penetrate. They can be dealt with easily by regular use of chemical or organic sprays. It is a good idea, if you use chemical sprays, to use a number of different products in rotation so as to eliminate those not susceptible to one type or another. Many people are opposed to using such sprays and there are many good organic products on the market. These use natural 'soaps' in their constituents and clog up the insects' spiracles (external respiratory openings) and so suffocate them.

Scale Insects

The scale insects have two life stages, one mobile and one immobile. They are seen as small, immobile insects that produce a limpet-like brown 'shell' on the leaves of plants, generally on their undersides. Beneath its shell the adult is busy sucking away at your plant. Beneath other shells are the maturing eggs that will hatch into the mobile stage. On hatching they move off to colonize new leaves and other plants. When they settle on a spot they insert their proboscis and form the shell. Scale insects are a particularly difficult pest to get rid of because the shell is impervious to our chemical sprays. But they can be controlled by using a systemic preparation on a regular basis. The natural, soap-based products mentioned above are particularly effective against them.

If you have only a small outbreak on a single plant then I would suggest that you give it a thorough wash using a 25–75 per cent mixture of methylated spirit and water, making sure that all the plant is washed with the solution. By using an artist's paint brush you can get into all the little crevices around the plant. You can also use a soft toothbrush to scrub the leaves. You may need to brush fairly briskly since the scale clings tenaciously, but be careful not to brush too hard and damage the leaf.

Red Spider Mite

This can be a problem since it can build up large colonies before being detected. You will notice them first when your plant develops small, whitish patches on the leaves, and then you will observe a fine filigree of web over the plant. Red spider is usually a pest of the warm, dry greenhouse and not such a problem in the orchid house because of its humidity and the spraying being carried out. It will usually attack the thin-leaved varieties such as *Lycaste* or *Cymbidium*. By ensuring that you keep all your plants well sprayed with water you can discourage red spider. If you do get an attack use one of the organic or chemical sprays available from the garden centre.

Snails and Slugs

These are the big destroyers of new shoots and new flower buds; they can munch their way through a whole flower spike or new growth in a night. A lot of damage is caused by young snails and slugs since they are small enough to hide among the compost during the day and then come out at night to continue their ravaging. There are two ways in which to do battle against these molluscs. One is to conduct night-time visits to the greenhouse and pick them up either from the plants or from the glass where they graze the algae. The alternative is to use slug pellets and sprinkle these around the benches, on the floor and in the pots. There are also liquid preparations on the market that are sprayed around the pots and on the benches.

Ants

Ants are constantly searching for new food sources. They are attracted to orchids because they exude a sugary sap from the flower buds. If ants are allowed to continue their foraging unchecked they will begin to build their nests inside the pots of your plants. They will also encourage aphids and moulds, so in these situations they should be dealt with. There are several preparations available for dealing with them. On the other hand, they can be useful: if your culture allows you to mop-up all the sugary sap, thus depriving the ants of it, they will turn their attention to eating the moulds from the leaves of plants. Even so their populations need to be kept in check.

Cattleya *flower following a nocturnal visit by a snail or slug.*

Vine Weevil

This is a beetle whose population is all-female. As such, it does do not need to mate, but it produces large numbers of eggs which are laid in the compost of many pot plants, and orchids are no exception. If you notice semi-circular pieces cut from petals or leaves, this is a sure sign of their presence. They hide in the compost during the day and forage at night. The adult will disfigure a plant but may not kill it. It is the larvae that cause most damage. They eat the roots of the plant and you will not notice the problem until it is too late, when the top growth begins to die. There are organic methods of control in the form of nematodes. They infest the vine weevil larvae, ultimately killing them. The adults are more difficult to get rid of, hence the concentration on the larval stage. Vigilance and night-time foraging yourself may also help to keep them in check.

Woodlice

These are familiar enough and will be seen as common creatures in the garden and in many greenhouses beneath pieces of debris or in pots where they thrive on decomposing organic matter. Woodlice and the larvae of many invertebrates are simply doing what they are intended to do, to breakdown dead organic matter, which in the wild helps to recycle leaves and other matter, ultimately turning them into soil. Because we orchid growers use much organic material such as bark and moss in our composts, woodlice are naturally attracted to it. If they get into the pots they will hasten the decomposition of the compost and they may even turn their attention to young roots. The best way to avoid them infesting the greenhouse is to practise good hygiene. In a greenhouse with a solid floor keep this free of all pots, bags, boxes and so on. A high standard of cleanliness and hygiene may be achieved by regular sweeping and cleaning with water and Jeyes Fluid. Be careful using Jeyes Fluid near plants. It is a strong substance and it will harm orchids, especially epiphytic roots. In a greenhouse with a natural floor woodlice are more difficult to get rid of and the only thing you can do to discourage them is to keep the greenhouse floor as clean as possible.

Bees and Butterflies

These will enter the greenhouse, but they are really more of a problem than a pest. The large bumblebees, of which many are protected, may inadvertently damage flowers when visiting in search of pollen because of their size. This may be a problem in the spring when the queen bee emerges from hibernation and is looking for food and a bright cymbidium may prove too much of an attraction. The remedy is to prevent access by all insects with the use of a screen that covers the door and any vents. It may also save their lives as they may become trapped in the greenhouse and die. By preventing access you will also prevent them from laying their eggs on your plants and the hatching caterpillars from eating them.

Moss Flies

These are very small creatures that have difficulty in flying and tend to move around the surface of the compost, but, as with many insects, it is the larvae that cause the problems. Living beneath the surface of the compost they are seldom seen. Because of their size, moss flies can build up into large populations quickly. Their larvae will help to quicken the decomposition of the compost and they may eat small young roots. The adults are easily killed with a standard insecticide. The larvae live deep within the compost and they are more difficult to destroy, but flushing the pot through with water containing an insecticide can kill them. The problem is breaking their life cycle, as with most pests, but by regular treatment and vigilance you should keep you greenhouse relatively free from pests.

Mice and Rats

In the winter, when it is cold outdoors and food is scarce for many animals, you may be visited by mice, who will be searching for food and shelter especially in a warm orchid house. Mice can be destructive in their foraging and nest-building operations. They will dig up the compost in their search and gnaw stems and pseudobulbs. They like pollen and they may chew through electric cabling. To deter them, cleanliness is again foremost; do not store bird food in the greenhouse which may attract them. Keep doors and windows closed and ensure that they have a tight fit. It may be a good idea also to have a metal strip attached to the base of the door to prevent mice from gnawing their way through. If you think that mice are present then you should set traps for them. Humane traps that will catch them live are available, but then you will have to move them far away, which can pose another problem. Their large cousin the rat can do even more damage than mice.

Organic Methods of Pest Control

I have mentioned organic insecticidal sprays above. In Britain look out for the Henry Doubleday Research Association (HDRA) logo as a symbol for organic products. Apart from sprays there are insect predators that can be introduced in a greenhouse. This predator–prey method of controlling pests is now well developed and used by many orchid growers. The ways in which the predators control the pests vary, some just eat their prey, while others parasitize a host. The types of predator range from small wasps, to species of ladybird and to nematode worms. Some of these may be available from the larger garden centres, but the most likely supplier would be the specialist. For their addresses I suggest the classified advertisements of a good gardening magazine.

Some years ago the journal *Lindleyana* of the American Orchid Society recommended a mixture containing detergent and vegetable oil in the ratio of 2:1 tablespoons to a (US) gallon of warm water. Use this to wash your plant of any pest, but a word of warning: do not overdo the oil; I think that it is better to use slightly under the ratio mentioned or a coating will be left on the plants that attracts mould. It does clean up the plants and a wipe over the treated plants with clean, warm water will remove the dead scale and any surplus oil.

If you put a drop or two of normal washing-up liquid in a misting hand sprayer this will also help to keep down aphids and the like. Do not overdo the detergent, you will need only a very small amount.

A way to trap crawling and many flying insects is to place among your orchids some pots of insectivorous plants such as butterwort (*Pinguicula*) or sundew (*Drosera*) and possibly also a pitcher plant (*Sarracenia*). These are effective at catching insects and they look attractive as well. Stand them in a saucer of rainwater, do not feed them and use a non-calcareous (acid) soil with them.

CULTURAL PROBLEMS

When you look around at your plants, you may notice that the leaves have spots, blemishes, scorch marks, moulds, or are twisted or folded concertina-like. Whatever the mark or blemish the problem could be put down to poor culture, a plant being in the wrong place, too close to the glass or it may be in need of repotting. This section will give you some idea as to the cause of those non-pest problems.

To deal with these problems equip yourself with an orchid first-aid kit which should have in it:

- a small knife with a pointed blade;
- a razor blade (a dissecting type with a handle) or a scalpel;
- a tub of yellow sulphur;
- a bottle containing a 25–75 per cent mixture of methylated spirit and water;
- an artist's paint brush, small size;
- a soft-bristled toothbrush;
- a small bottle of alcohol (ethanol);
- a lighter to flame the blades with before cutting (after immersing them in the alcohol).

Roots Outside the Pot

This is a case of simple neglect and repotting is the solution. Plants such as *Cattleya* and *Phalaenopsis* are prone to this problem. Cattleyas grow on a long rhizome and quickly extend over the side of the pot. Many growers mount cattleyas on bark and their roots are naturally open to the atmosphere, which is part of their natural habit. *Phalaenopsis* are monopodial and produce roots from several points up their stem above the compost.

Do not worry too much about these aerial roots, they do not constitute a major catastrophe, many orchids do this; keep them sprayed on a daily basis, adding a dilute liquid feed to the water and all will be fine until you can repot the plants. Roots outside the pot may be placed back into compost during the

Lycaste.

next repotting session. Do not attempt to put them back by bending them because they will only snap. During the repotting the roots will be prone to damage and it may be wise to shorten them before doing so; nevertheless, care should be taken not to damage them further. Knock the plant from its pot and remove any dead roots; the older back-bulbs may be removed or the whole plant may be potted-on if it is growing well all round.

Dead Roots

These may be a sign of overwatering, prolonged drought or infrequent repotting. They may be an indication of other problems, such as too high a fertilizer concentration or the use of softened or treated water. Whatever the cause, the end result may well be the death of the plant, but you may be able to save it. The initial remedy is to remove all the dead roots and the old compost. You should repot into fresh compost, keep the plant sprayed with water but do not water the compost. You should resume watering only when the new roots are well established. Now take a critical look at your culture and ask yourself, 'What am I doing wrong? Am I watering too often, am I using fertilizer at too high a concentration, is the water suitable?' When you have determined the cause, alter your culture in order to prevent the problem from happening again.

Leaf Scorch

This is a problem caused by the sun shining through the glass. The problem is made worse if there is too little shading and low humidity inside the greenhouse. The leaves will become dry, they will be discoloured (yellow, black and brown), with patches usually at those points closest to the window. What you need to do is install or increase the shading and increase the cooling and/or the humidity (*see* Chapters 6 and 7).

It may also be a problem caused by insecticides, if their concentrations are too high, and it may occur if you use unsuitable products or mix two products. You should always read the labels on chemical products to determine whether there are any exclusions. Talk to other growers or nursery staff for advice and on the successes or problems they may have encountered. The remedy here is to look carefully at your methods and culture. When using two different substances to control pests do not use them together, spray each on a separate day, try using lower dilutions, different products or consider organic methods.

Leaf Reddening

This is generally attributed to excessive light, poor root condition or insufficient nitrogen, or it may be a combination of these. The remedy is to apply sufficient shading, have a look at the condition of the roots and assure yourself that you are using enough feed at the correct dilution and often enough.

Leaf Yellowing

This is known as chlorosis and can be put down either to the distress of the plant or to some other reason: excessive light, poor feeding, lack of essential nutrients, root damage, or it may simply be the die-back of old leaves. This is another case for assessing your culture; ask yourself whether you are watering and feeding consistently during the growing season? Are you repotting at the right time?

Flower Bud Drop

This may be attributed to more than one cause. It may be too much heat, so check the thermostat of your heater. It may be that the gas heater is burning poorly. Have it serviced and get the burners checked because the unburnt gases in the air may be the problem. It could be poor ventilation, thus causing a build up of unburnt gases; it could possibly be the result of fires being close by and the fumes or smoke from them entering the greenhouse. An excess of ethylene will make the buds drop. Decaying flowers also produce ethylene and so remove these.

Weeds

There are many other plants that will also like the environment of the orchid house, some of them you may have introduced intentionally to enhance your displays, such as ferns or begonias, others will have come in as seed from one source or another. If you are presenting plants for showing and there are weeds in the pots, you will lose points for poor culture. *Ferns* grow well in the damp, warm conditions of the orchid house; they are a problem because they will take up food and water intended for the orchids. Their roots will compete for space in the pot and will eventually completely fill it to the detriment of the orchid. *Oxalis* is a small plant with shamrock-like leaves and yellow flowers. It grows long stolons (horizontal stems that root at points along their length, forming new plants) beneath the compost and spreads quickly through these. It also has explosive dehiscent seedpods by which means it can spread

Stanhopea occulatum.

rapidly throughout the greenhouse. Again, the problem is that it competes for water and feed. *Algae* may be seen on the sides of terracotta pots and possibly over the surface of compost; in both cases it is a sure sign of conditions being too wet. Algae on the surface of the compost may be caused by an organic fertilizer, such as dried blood, but even so algae need wet conditions to thrive, but an over-wet compost is bad for orchids. *Moss* and *lichen*, as with algae, live in damp conditions; you may well have moss growing on the brickwork or woodwork, but should you have it your pots the compost is again too wet and a change in watering method is urgently needed.

Many of the problems considered here, it will be seen, are the result of poor culture. It is important in order to achieve your goal and grow fine plants that you attempt to standardize and eliminate those areas that give you problems. Endeavour to regulate your routines, adopt some automation, enjoy your plants and, if you look at them closely, you will spot problems early and, with vigilance, can prevent many of them from developing into catastrophes. My advice would be not to use herbicides to rid yourself of weeds such as those mentioned above.

DISEASES ASSOCIATED WITH ORCHIDS

Plant disease is sometimes better treated by disposing of the affected plants by burning them. But if you have a large specimen plant or a special one then you will want to do all you can to nurture it back to health. Many diseases are spread by insects and other pests, so if you can keep these in check then the potential disease problem is going to be lessened.

Bacterial Problems

These usually manifest themselves in the form of scabs, blisters or blotches on the leaves or pseudobulbs. It is uncertain how a plant is infected but it is most likely via an insect or some other pest, snail or slug. Preventive measures, such as pest control, good culture, plant and glasshouse hygiene, are probably the best course of action to prevent an attack. If you do have a plant that is infected then you should remove it at once since an insect can quickly pass on the problem to other plants.

Any plants being treated should ideally be separated from the others and kept in a place where the humidity is reduced. To treat an infected plant cut off the infected leaf or lance the blister on the infected 'bulb' and remove all infected matter from the wound by using the first-aid kit described at the beginning of this chapter. When you have cleaned the wound, the plant should be dried by standing it in front of a fan, then treated with yellow sulphur which acts as an antiseptic. If the infection is on a pseudobulb then the area can be cut out and all infected matter removed until you come to good tissue. Again treat the area with yellow sulphur.

While the plant is recovering reduce watering and raise the pH to a little more than the neutral range 7–7.2. This can be done by adding dolomite lime to the compost surface. The reason for this is because the commonest cause of problems is *Erwinia* which cannot tolerate alkalinity. It is also a good idea to keep the temperature a little warmer, with a night temperature of around 20°C (68°F).

You are always advised that prevention is better than cure and so a twice-yearly spray using a fungicide is a good measure (*Erwinia* does not like fungicide either). Spray all round the benches, pots and plants, covering all surfaces within the greenhouse. Hygiene and cleanliness are vital and, as mentioned earlier, remove all dead plant material, keep the floor clear and remember that insects transfer diseases, including viruses. If you see any suspect plant, remove it and quarantine it for a few weeks. If you do get an infected plant the only sure way to deal with it is to destroy it by burning, as you can never be absolutely sure that the virus will not return.

Fungal Problems

These can be dealt with relatively easily with an application of a commercial fungicide which will clear the problem quickly. But they are likely to return at some stage and on each occasion will spoil leaves, creating brown spots and looking so unsightly that you will not be able to show any affected plant. Thus you need to build up resistance within the plants by applying liquid silicon and humic acid on a regular basis.

CHAPTER 12

Repotting and Containers

Repotting can be a worry for the beginner to orchid growing but should not be. Those of you who grow houseplants do not worry about repotting your other plants and so you should not worry about repotting your orchids. I think it may be because orchids look unusual and have a different root system from 'normal' plants. In horticulture timing is all-important for many things and the repotting of orchids is no exception.

The main reason for repotting so is to replace compost that has deteriorated because, if this is not done, it will have an effect on the health of the roots. It is also a time at which to assess the health of the plant generally, as well as the roots and to decide whether cultural changes should be made. From being new, bark-based orchid composts will deteriorate over a period of eighteen months to two years. This will depend very much on the watering and feeding regime. It is not a good idea though to wait until you are forced to repot because the compost will then be in such a state that it will begin to suffocate the epiphytic roots. Always remember that orchid roots need a lot of air and, as the compost rots, it will become more and more dense and lack air. The frequency of repotting also depends on the species; those that grow quickly and grow out of the pot will need to be put back in it more often, every year perhaps. The process of repotting causes stress in the plant and some genera do not take kindly to it and will sulk for some time and not flower again for at least a season. It is important therefore to select carefully the timing of your repotting session. There is an optimum time during the growth cycle of each genus when it will cause the least stress (*see* Chapter 14). Generally the ideal time is spring. This in Britain can be any time between February and April depending on genus.

THE REPOTTING PROCESS

An important rule to remember is: *do not over-pot.* That is to say, do not repot your plant into too large a pot because the compost will remain too wet for too long and will cause root rot; it will also hasten decomposition of the compost. If you are simply potting-on, that is, putting your plant into a larger pot because its present one is too small, then select one that is only one or two sizes larger.

Hygiene is also very important during this process in order to reduce the likelihood of spreading any infection. Before you begin, give the plant a check over and assess its health; an unhealthy plant may not be worth repotting and is best disposed of, or it may be in need of further treatment. Check that the plant is free from pests and also disease-free. Do not worry if you have an unhealthy plant, some losses are inevitable and tolerable as long as the rest are in good health.

Equipment

- A stout, strong-bladed knife;
- a pair of secateurs;
- a large bin or sack for the debris;
- ethanol and a spirit lamp to sterilize the blades;
- sufficient compost or composts for the purpose;
- plenty of clean pots;
- a box for the used pots;
- space to work in.

Collect together on a clean, suitable bench all your tools and equipment. You may also need a bucket of warm water with added Physan, a sterilizing agent suitable for use with orchids. This is to wash all the pots that you will need; better still, you could have pots ready newly washed. For the sake of your plants do not reuse an unwashed pot and do not remove a plant from one pot and put a different plant into it. The chances of spreading the eggs of pests or infectious bacteria will be eliminated if you use fresh, clean pots.

The cutting tools should be sterilized following the repotting of one plant and before moving on to the next. Wipe off any plant material with a cloth, stand the blade (knife or secateurs) in ethanol for a minute and them flame it by using the spirit lamp.

The compost is easier to use and less dusty if it has been dampened. Wet the compost the night before your repotting operation and place it to drain in the greenhouse so that it can attain the same temperature as your plants. To drain a large amount of compost, have a dustbin with a garden sieve in the bottom. Before you begin the repotting give the compost a good mix up to ensure that the ingredients are evenly distributed and to aerate it.

The Process

1. Take the plant you are to repot and, working over a bin, remove it from the pot. If the roots are stuck to the sides of a plastic pot you may be able to loosen them by squeezing the outside of it. Otherwise take a long-bladed knife and run it around the inside of the pot.
2. Put that pot into a box to separate it from the clean ones.
3. Remove all the old compost, teasing it out from inside the root-ball. Handle the plant carefully so as not to damage the roots and any new growths that may be present.
4. Check the roots and cut off all the obviously dead ones. These will be soft and brown; they will come away easily when pulled.
5. Live roots will feel firm when squeezed gently between finger and thumb, they will also be of a lighter colour. Some of these roots may be very long, having wound themselves around the inside of the pot, these may be shortened by one-third, by doing so they will be easier to accommodate in their new pot.
6. Remove any old flower spikes and dead or dying leaves. Also remove the brown, papery sheathing from the older pseudobulbs and check for the presence of pests; they tend to hide in these

The process is quite simple, but you will need to make one or two decisions as you go on. The first will be whether to divide the plant or not. If the plant has bare pseudobulbs in its centre I suggest that you divide it into two. Otherwise just pot it on into a slightly larger pot. The following sequence will guide you through the dividing and repotting of a cymbidium.

Stage 1: *gather the clean pots, wetted compost and all the tools you need – detailed instructions are in the text.*

Stage 2: *knock the plant from its pot. This may be difficult because cymbidiums like to be slightly pot-bound and may therefore be difficult to budge; terracotta pots may break during this process.*

Stage 3: *look at the plant and decide whether to divide it or not. Cut about a third of the roots away with secateurs. Work tidily and put all debris in a bin so as to keep the work area clear.*

places. But be careful in doing this near last season's growth because the new growths will be forming beneath these protective sheaths and are easily broken. It may be wise to leave the bracts around the more recent pseudobulbs for this reason.

7. Select the new pot and place into it some drainage material and/or ballast. Now position the plant so as to give it room to grow. Take a good look at the plant and check where the new growths are emerging. You need to do this in order that you may give the new growth plenty of room to develop, therefore do not put them against the side of the pot thus restricting their development. The drainage material used is usually broken pieces of polystyrene, or gravel or broken terracotta pot, if you need something with more weight.

Stage 4: *with a sharp knife cut through the short rhizomes, thus dividing the plant. Before you cut, follow an obvious route through the plant with your fingers to decide where to cut.*

Stage 5: *when you have severed the plant you will see that there are not many live roots in the ball if the plant has not been repotted for a number of years. The one shown has not been repotted for many years and is in desperate need of rejuvenation.*

8. When you are satisfied that the plant will have room to develop, gently fill the pot with the new compost, easing it between the roots with your fingers and being careful not to damage the roots further.
9. The rhizomes of sympodial orchids (cattleyas) should be slightly buried beneath the new compost. With successive waterings this will compact a little and the rhizomes will attain their correct position.
10. With some of the taller plants you may need to provide a stake after the repotting in order to help the plant to stand upright. Use a green-coloured split cane pushed in alongside one of the taller growths, then, with string or a length of twist-tie wire, fasten this growth to the cane.

Stage 6: *the dead roots need to be teased out, and also tease out old compost. The plant shown has many dead roots; these are obvious because they feel 'empty' and their outer covering will pull away easily, leaving the fine inner core. Live roots will feel solid. New roots will appear white and have a greenish end. Some roots may be dead along part of their length and these may be cut back to where they are live. Very long roots may be shortened.*

Stage 7: *the plant will benefit, visually, by your cleaning away the old bracts from around the pseudobulbs. Be careful when doing this because these bracts act as a protective sheath for the developing new shoots, which break off easily. The risk of damaging new growth is the reason for repotting before it begins to develop.*

11. Do not forget to replace the label or to provide a correctly named one.
12. In the period following the repotting you will need to allow time for the wounds caused by root trimming or dividing to heal over. The compost used should have been damp, and, in order to allow cuts to heal, you should not water the plant for a least two or three weeks. After this you may slowly begin to water normally. If, on the other hand, you only potted the plant on into a larger container and did not disturb the roots, then normal watering may continue. You should, however, keep the leaves sprayed to prevent excessive transpiration and dehydration while the plant is producing new roots.

Stage 8: *place into the bottom of the pot some drainage material. I have used broken polystyrene here but you could use pebbles, broken brick or large-grade bark. The pots should be clean. If you use old pots give them a thorough wash with disinfectant in the water. Physan is ideal for this; allow the pots to air-dry before using them.*

Stage 9: *when you position the plant in the pot make sure that the lead shoot has room to develop. The plant should be placed centrally if you are unsure whence the lead may develop. In essence, the plant needs room to grow outwards. There may, of course, be more than one site of new growth. When you have positioned the plant, fill in the pot with the new compost and gradually fill and firm the compost until the pot is full. If you have done this properly you should be able to lift the plant gently by its leaves and pick up the whole pot.*

Stage 10: *the completed job, with two well repotted cymbidiums ready for the summer's growing. When you have repotted them do not forget to label them. You could include on the label, apart from the plant name, details such as the repotting date. Some people also use a code, cross-referenced to a file card where details of the culture and the state of the plant at repotting time are kept. It will need time for the plant to recover from the shock that you have just given it; it should therefore be placed somewhere cool and shady. Do not water it for about a week, the damp compost will be sufficient. Any pseudobulbs that have been removed during repotting may be potted up and put in a similar place. Keep the compost just moist and wait for new growth to appear.*

TYPES OF POT AND CONTAINER

The choice here is an important consideration in the cultivation of orchids. They are grown in plastic or terracotta pots, in hanging baskets of various designs, or they may be fastened on to pieces of cork-oak bark. Traditionally, it was the terracotta pot that dominated simply because there was no alternative, but there was for orchids a particular type with extra holes in its bottom and sides in order to increase the air supply to the roots. This type of pot is uncommon in cultivation these days, though they are attractive and orchids grow well in them. You may be able to get them specially made. Today the terracotta pot is still with us, but the plastic pot dominates the market. The question is, which to choose? Is one better than another? Both have their drawbacks and one is related to the watering regime you need to adopt. The terracotta pot, being a natural product, will absorb moisture from the compost and this will evaporate from the outside of the pot; the inside will therefore be cooler and dry more quickly. The plastic pot, on the other hand, is impervious to moisture and, as a result, remains wetter for longer. Black plastic pots, although used by many orchid growers, absorb heat and will warm up inside them, which may not suit the roots, but I have heard of no reports of adverse affects due to the use of black pots. You can, of course, drill or burn (with a soldering iron) extra holes in the sides and base of plastic pots. Because terracotta pots are hard and brittle it is difficult to drill holes through them, and I would not even try. The cool growing species grow well in terracotta because these are cooler inside. A recent innovation has been the introduction of transparent, plastic pots. These are normally, and successfully, used for *Phalaenopsis* because these plants photosynthesize through their roots as well as their leaves.

Conventional pots, either terracotta or plastic, are not the only containers in which you can grow orchids.

TOP RIGHT: *Hanging sleeve made from plastic netting.*

RIGHT: *Victorian terracotta pot (notice the extra holes in the sides for increased air circulation and drainage).*

A plastic net-pot holding a Stanhopea.

A Maxillaria *mounted on cork bark.*

The roots of some orchids, *Phalaenopsis* and cattleyas in particular, tend to cling tenaciously to any surface they come into contact with, as they would on tree branches in the wild. This is equally true of the inside of terracotta pots and at repotting time they are almost impossible to remove without damaging their roots. Plastic pots can be manipulated from the outside by squeezing and pressing the sides; this sometimes loosens roots because they cannot cling so well to plastic, thus causing less damage to them as they are removed.

One other point against plastic pots is that they are light in weight. Many orchids are top-heavy and so without ballast in the pot they do tend to topple over even with the lightest of touches, thus requiring emergency repotting. If they do topple over, the fall may break off new growths or flower spikes. To overcome this problem you can place in the bottom of the pot some stones or a piece of brick to counterbalance the top weight of the orchid. For a large plant you could stand the plastic pot inside a larger, heavier, terracotta or stone pot.

Hanging Baskets

Many orchids do not like to have their roots enclosed in pots and grow less well as a result. The solution in this case is to grow them in a hanging basket. The traditional hanging basket for orchids is made from teak and allows the roots to grow out into the atmosphere of the greenhouse. These are produced in several sizes from 10cm (4in) up to 20cm (8in) and because they are fabricated from teak they have an extremely long life.

Another pattern one may use is the equally traditional floral hanging basket. These wire baskets are large 20cm (8in) up to 40cm (16in) and can accommodate the larger clump-forming orchids. *Stanhopea* do well in these because of their habit of sending their inflorescences downwards. I have found *Coelogyne* also do well because they do not like disturbance and they can be grown to a considerable size without the need for repotting. These baskets allow free drainage and plenty of air can get to the roots; they simulate the epiphyte's natural habitat. By using an automatic watering system in association with hanging baskets they can be kept uniformly moist. There are also plastic versions of hanging baskets available.

An orchid display using the floral hanging basket, as normally used for summer bedding displays. It makes an excellent container for orchids.

Alternative Forms of Pot

I have quite successfully used a type of pot that is intended for aquatic plants; these are available in garden centres with water garden departments. You can also purchase, from orchid sundries dealers, plastic pots known as net-pots; these are made from thick plastic and are a type of hanging basket with slotted sides. Net pots are available in several sizes from 6cm (2½in) to 14cm (5½in). Both these types have very open sides, either with many small slits (aquatic pots) or with large, net-like slits (net pots). Both do the same job in that they allow plenty of air to get to the roots.

The use of seed-trays, either full or half-size, may be useful for some genera that grow long rhizomes and would therefore be almost impossible to retain in a pot. They are shallow and therefore do not hold much compost; they have plenty of drainage holes and allow the compost to dry out reasonably quickly.

Moss poles may be useful for species that grow vertically; some species of *Coelogyne* tend to do this, *C. ocellata*, *C. fuscescens* and *C. cristata*, for instance. When using moss poles you will need to provide copious amounts of water and automation comes in here. There is an alternative to the moss pole that I devised myself and is easy to make, I call it a hanging sleeve. Garden centres will sell you plastic netting intended for fencing; this is either green or brown in colour, has a mesh size of about 1cm square and is supplied by length. To make a sleeve you will need to cut a rectangular piece of the net of about sixteen by twenty-five squares. You will also need some twist-tie wire, a short length of stout wire (to form a hook) and some peat-based orchid compost. To form the sleeve fold the net and, by using the twist-tie wire, fasten two opposing edges and one end together. The sleeve can now be filled with the compost, firming it as you fill (but not too much). When it is filled, tie up the open end. Now thread the stouter wire through the mesh at one end, bend it over to prevent it from slipping out and bend the other end into a hook by which to hang it up. Soak the sleeve in water and allow to drain. It is now ready for you to attach your plant to it. Fasten the plant close to the bottom; this will give it space to climb up and around the sleeve. It is convenient to attach an automatic watering system to the sleeves.

CHAPTER 13

Types of Compost

In the past 200 years or so the development of orchid compost has gone through many changes. The local availability of suitable products usually dictates what is used. As such, there are many types of 'compost' used for orchid cultivation. I have orchids grown in pots containing broken volcanic lava or some other lightweight stone. The Victorian gardener used osmunda fibre, which is the root mass from the fern *Osmunda regalis*, a British native species but now quite rare because of this practice, but orchids seem to be amenable to a wide range of compost products.

Orchid compost should have the following qualities:

- retain sufficient water without being over-wet;
- remain open when wet;
- hold a large volume of air;
- be slow to deteriorate;
- have sufficient structure to hold the plant in the pot;
- be readily available;
- be reasonably priced.

BARK

Bark is the preferred compost for many growers. The material is a by-product of the timber industry, the source being the Corsican pine or a similar tree since it has a hard bark. What makes it so suitable is that it is slow to decompose. When I began growing orchids this was the 'traditional' compost, available in variously sized pieces. The size or grade of the bark compost used depended on the genus being grown. Generally, the finer the orchid root the finer the grade of bark one used; for example, cattleyas have rather thick roots and in the wild grow in places where drainage is perfect and there is plenty of air around the roots, and therefore a coarse bark would be used. The *Odontoglossum* orchids have finer roots and therefore one would use a finer grade of bark. Seedlings are planted in a still finer grade. The bark would customarily have been mixed with other ingredients to provide a material that held enough water yet was open, drained well and was airy, thus providing the orchid roots with an environment as close to that found in their natural habitat as possible.

Unfortunately, over recent years it has became less readily available from its original source in France, but new sources are being sought and so it can still be obtained (*see* the Appendices). It is a good, all-round compost and available ready-mixed or as bark and in several grade sizes. If you purchase your compost unmixed there are several products available together with other materials that you can add to the bark, such as perlite or pumice (which will retain water); charcoal (which helps to keep the compost in good condition as it absorbs salts); horticultural foam (another water-retaining material); and sphagnum moss (or moss used for floral hanging baskets). The usual mixture is bark, charcoal and perlite in the ratio of 5:1:1.

The bark-based compost is still used by many growers, but in recent years other types have become available; these are considered separately.

COIR

This is the fibre from the outer husk of the coconut and is a good medium for orchids. It holds a reasonable amount of water yet is open, thus allowing air into the mix. Coir can be included with other ingredients to provide suitable composts for the

Some of the many materials in which to grow epiphytic orchids. The terrestrial types could use some of these with the addition of a soil-based compost. From top right clockwise: cork-bark raft, lump peat with horticultural foam, sphagnum moss, large-grade bark, medium-grade bark with charcoal and perlite (ready mixed compost), Hortag expanded clay granules, Seramis terracotta granules, and volcanic ash.

various genera or used alone. You do need to treat it before use though. It is usually stored at the docks in the open before being shipped and is therefore subject to salt spray from the sea. All you need to do is soak it for 24hr then get rid of this water and give it a rinse through with clean water. Allow it to drain for another 24hr and it is ready to use. If you have a conductivity meter you can check the salt content or, to be absolutely sure, you can give it another soaking. It is usually purchased through orchid nurseries or sundries suppliers.

GRANULATED CORK

This is sold as a long-lasting compost for use with cattleyas. It is available in largish pieces, is light, easy to use and does not necessarily need any additional ingredients, though you may choose to do so.

CORK PIECES AND CORK TRUNKS

These are useful for fastening those plants that do not like to have their roots enclosed within pots, but this is not their only use. Many genera can be fastened to cork rafts, they look more realistic in this way and I like to see plants growing in more natural settings. The trunks make good additions to displays either at shows or in the greenhouse. If you can get a plant to cover a large trunk it looks impressive. You will need to place a pad of moss or coir between the plant and the bark as a material that will hold some moisture.

FERN FIBRE

This is produced from the trunks of tree ferns and is a renewable product, because the growing part of tree ferns is at the top of the plants. They can therefore be cut, the top section replanted and the rest of the trunk used to provide growers with useful products. Fern fibre is usually supplied cut into blocks which can be divided further with a sharp knife. It is usually cut into slabs to suit the plant that is to be fastened to it. Some growers fix pieces of fern fibre on to cork bark slabs and the plants on to these. The beauty of fern fibre is that it drains freely and is suitable for those genera that do not like their roots to remain wet for any length of time. These genera would experience a thorough drenching, the roots would absorb what water they could and the substrate would drain quickly.

LEAF MOULD AND GARDEN COMPOST

These are used as compost ingredients for many terrestrial orchids, along with perlite, grit, medium/fine bark and charcoal. The mixture is designed to retain moisture but drains well. In many books you may read that the compost should have perfect drainage. This means that the plant does not like to be constantly wet, therefore the compost should have enough coarse material to allow water to drain away quickly but it should still hold sufficient to remain moist.

SERAMIS AND HORTAG

The product known as Seramis is crushed terracotta and is sold as a compost ingredient for terrestrial orchids, but I see no reason why it would not be a suitable compost for a wider range of genera. Again, I see no reason why orchids cannot be grown in the expanded clay granules known in Britain as Hortag. This is sold as drainage material or to cover deep benches and to stand pots on. The beauty of these two products is that they do not rot and, being inorganic, will last many years. I think that they could be reused, and at repotting time the dead plant roots can be removed, the material cleaned and sterilized before being reused. I have used Seramis with *Dendrobium kingianum* and it has grown successfully, producing large pseudobulbs and flowering well. Experiment a little and try out new or different composts.

ADDITIVES

Associated with bark-based composts are certain additives used to alter the pH of the compost. These are calcium nitrate ($CaNO_3$) and dolomitic limestone ($CaMg(CO_3)_2$); both are intended to raise the pH. Bark, as it decomposes, becomes acidic, but with the addition of limestone (alkaline) as a top dressing the compost will remain closer to a neutral or slightly higher value. Not all orchids would benefit from such treatment because most epiphytes experience acidic conditions among decomposing organic matter. Those plants that grow lithophytically on limestone, however, would gain from a top-dressing of either of these materials.

Whichever compost you choose it is a good idea to have all your plants in a similar type of compost. By doing this you will learn how it 'works' and how much and how often to water and feed.

CHAPTER 14

The Orchid Year, Season by Season

In every branch of horticulture, as the year passes, one should be looking to certain aspects of culture and orchids are no exception. In this chapter I detail some of the tasks you should be attending to. Obviously, there will be differences in the timing of certain jobs depending on your geographical location. Here you will need to take into account those aspects of the weather that influence plant growth and to remember that in the greenhouse growth occurs much earlier than outdoors. You will have to watch the day length, the rising temperature and the sun's intensity. So, we shall begin with spring when new growth is beginning.

SPRING

This is the time at which you will be checking for new growth. At this time you need to ensure that the plants are getting enough water. But be careful when watering, because if you allow water to hold in the new growths it will cause these tender new shoots to rot, and do not get the compost too wet either, because this may also cause rotting at the base of the new shoots. You can begin to feed at this time, but apply it in only very dilute concentrations (a quarter of the recommended strength). This will be increased as the growth increases and the roots extend. Another reason for not getting the compost too wet at this time is to encourage the roots to grow down into the compost and search for water. If the compost is too wet they will not develop properly. The sun's intensity is increasing from now on and so now you can begin to think about shading, although it may not be required all the time. Where I live in the north of England I cannot rely on the sun shining from one day to the next. You may therefore apply a single layer of shading by using paint or shade cloth. As the summer advances additional shading can be put up. Plants indoors on the window sill will also need to be protected from the sun with the aid of net curtains, or you should move them below the sill out of the direct sun. At this time of the year repotting should be undertaken; this will also give you the opportunity to give your plants a good inspection and to assess the culture you gave them last year. Ask yourself whether you need to change anything. If a plant is in flower, wait until the flowers have faded before repotting, or cut the spike off and use it in a flower arrangement. Not all orchid flowers last when cut but cymbidiums certainly do.

SUMMER

This is the time when everything should be growing well. You should be watering and feeding regularly. Everything should have been repotted and left in peace to produce strong pseudobulbs. In northern Europe and similar regions all those plants that can go outdoors, such as cymbidiums and the cool-growing dendrobiums and *Coelogyne*, should be in the garden in a shady place. The feed may be increased from the very dilute concentrations of spring. Continue to use a high nitrogen feed because this will help until the growths are growing away well. You can then increase the dilution to half strength and apply every second or third watering; re-establish a more balanced feed as the season develops. The cymbidiums that are outdoors need to kept well watered and treated with a balanced feed at every other watering. They are hungry feeders, but use at only half the recommended strength.

When you place your orchids outdoors it is a good idea to raise them off the ground, on a table or a bench made of bricks and timber or even on upturned pots. This will help to prevent unwanted visitors such as worms, woodlice, slugs and snails from making their home among the roots. Raising the pots off the ground will also aid drainage; they will then not become waterlogged in wet weather. In warm, sunny weather the pots will dry fairly quickly and so regular watering is necessary. Keep an eye on the old pseudobulbs of *Cymbidium*; you should not allow these to shrivel. Regular spraying is also advisable and, especially in hot weather, this will keep the plants moist and cool; it will also discourage pests such as red spider mites which thrive in hot, dry conditions and are a particular problem on cymbidiums and *Lycaste*. Check the undersides of leaves regularly for these and other pests. Inside the greenhouse humidity needs to be maintained by damping down or by the use of automated misters. The plants mounted on bark will dry quickly and will need to be watered daily. Summer is also the time when pests proliferate and if you have vents open this will give them free access. Larger insects such as bees will get into the greenhouse, so by putting up screens with a fine mesh you will stop all but the very smallest from entering.

With the lengthening day and increasing temperatures, extra shading may now be put up. It is a good idea to fix the shading so that there is a space of at least 30cm (12in) between the greenhouse roof and the shading. This is to allow good air movement between the two; this is important because it will keep the temperature down within the greenhouse; you will notice a difference of several degrees between the inside and the outside. The maximum temperature for the orchid house should be 20–25°C (68–77°F); plants will die if these temperatures are exceeded and the ventilation and shading are insufficient. Maintaining a buoyant atmosphere in the greenhouse is also important; we have mentioned shade, but humidity and air movement are equally so. Damping down either manually or automatically is necessary. Have enough fans in the greenhouse to ensure that there are no spots of still air. In the humid conditions of the orchid house fungal problems could become a problem.

Those plants on the window sill should be kept misted. It is difficult to build up humidity indoors, but by standing them on a gravel tray and grouping others around them a microclimate can be maintained. Keep the gravel wet, but do not let the orchids sit in water; use an upturned saucer or pot to stand them on. The night temperature by now should not be a worry and so the heater should not be needed again until autumn. But do not wait for the cold weather to return: have your heater serviced now.

This time of year also brings the annual holidays, which also brings the problem of who is going to look after the plants. If you have an orchid-loving friend then all well and good, but if not, what do you do? If you have adequate shading installed, remember that shading positioned 30cm (12in) above the glass can reduce internal temperatures. Automatic misting will provide humidity and if you have watered your plants immediately before leaving them, then all should be well for a fortnight. If you do not have these misters, then you could set a seeping hose attached to a watering-timer (available from most garden centres). This will wet the floor on a daily basis so creating sufficient humidity. Keep the doors and vents closed as this will retain that vital humidity.

Keep an eye on pests and treat them as soon as they are spotted; they can get a hold very quickly at this time of year. If you are an organic gardener and use the predator–prey method of control, you should, before introducing the predators, reduce the pest populations by spraying with an organic product and allowing a short period to elapse. If you spray after the introduction of the predator, you will kill them as well.

Late summer brings in another change in the feeding programme. Now is the time to switch to a high potassium feed. By doing this you will encourage strong flower formation and growth ready for next spring.

AUTUMN

This marks the return to shortening days and cooler nights when light frosts may occur on high ground and at higher latitudes. The heater may need to be in operation and the thermostat will watch for those early morning temperature drops. By late summer or the beginning of autumn all shading should have been removed and stored away for the winter. However, local conditions will dictate the time at which to take it down. The plants from now on will need as much light as they can get.

Late summer, before the weather cools too much, is a good time to clean the glass on the inside of the greenhouse, when the plants may be placed outside for a short time as you do this. Clean the glass and remove algae by using a suitable algicide at dilute strength. Check the insulation and ensure that there are no places where draughts can get in.

It is also time to bring back into the greenhouse those plants that have spent the summer outdoors, but check them first for unwanted guests; tip the plant out of the pot to check for slugs, snails and suchlike. The *Pleione*s may be returned to the cold greenhouse and allowed to dry, once the leaves have dropped. When they are dry they may be removed from their current compost and placed in new.

You can continue to feed with the high potassium feed while the plants are still growing. Keep an eye on them and, as they begin to pass into their rest period, you should also begin to reduce watering and feeding.

Check the pseudobulbs, which should be fat and solid; for example, the spring-flowering *Coelogyne ochracea* should be at this stage. The bulbs should be chubby and rounded, including the older leafless bulbs. At the base of the new pseudobulb you will notice a papery bract that, when brown, indicates the growth is complete. If not, continue to water for a few more weeks until the bract dies off; there should also be no wrinkled skin on the older bulbs. Again, carry on watering until they are all fully swollen. Even though many *Coelogyne* require a dry rest, a daily spray may be carried out during the rest period to ensure that excessive shrivelling does not occur. In the wild they experience an early morning mist which carries moisture, but there is no rain. If you notice that a plant is still growing, then carry on watering, otherwise, ease off the watering and feeding.

By the middle and towards the end of autumn most of your plants should have completed their growth cycle. However, the warmer growers will continue to grow, although at a slower rate; for these, continue to water as and when required. During winter fungal growth may become apparent, especially if the compost is too wet. For this reason you must be careful when spraying, particularly in cool, dull weather. For those plants not requiring a dry rest between waterings, you should give the compost time to dry before watering again. You may, from time to time, give a little feed at dilute concentrations, say a quarter strength.

WINTER

This is the time when there is not much happening and you can sit back and enjoy those plants in flower. Many are in their rest period and so watering has now ceased altogether or needs to be applied only occasionally. Any misting should only be done on sunny days. By spraying on dull, cool days you may encourage rot in the axils of the leaves (*see* above).

Pleione is one plant that will not need watering until just after flowering, the time when the new pseudobulb is forming. Others such as the cool growing *Coelogyne* will retain their leaves and do not want a totally dry rest. Some water needs to be given occasionally in order to keep the bulbs swollen. *Coelogyne* will also benefit by being misted; this helps to maintain swollen bulbs. Other orchids are still growing during the winter, albeit slowly; *Phalaenopsis*, *Miltoniopsis* and some of the *Odontoglossum* alliance are making pseudobulbs in winter. These plants need careful watering, but at a reduced level from that applied during the summer; give water only when the compost has dried out, but do not wait until it is bone dry, keep it barely moist. You may give a little feed also, but only at a quarter strength once a month until growth becomes more vigorous in the spring.

Similar treatment can be used on the *Vanda*s, which also continue to grow all the year round. Many of the intermediate and warm genera also continue to grow all the year round, and so careful watering is needed to keep them going. Meters are available that measure the moisture in the pots, but these are really designed for plants growing in soil and may not work as well in the open, bark-based composts used for orchids. Another method is to insert a dry stick into the compost, leave it a minute or two, take it out and feel the stick to see how wet it is. But I think the best way is to judge by the weight of the pot.

At this time of year the strength of the sun will not harm your plants so many can sit in direct sunlight. The more sun the better since it will induce flowering.

Keep an eye on your heater and watch the temperature, both inside the greenhouse and outside. Do not be caught out by a sudden fall in temperature and note the weather forecasts for your locality. You may need to adjust the thermostat slightly in very cold weather to maintain the greenhouse temperature.

Some plants will be forming flower spikes ready for the spring and you should be training these as they lengthen by tying them to split canes. You are well advised to tie them loosely at first to give them room to expand to their full width. If you tie them tightly they will swell and the wire will cut into the spikes, causing them to break off at the wire. To tie the spike, cut one end of the cane to a point and insert it just behind the flower spike. You may then tie it in as the spike develops; by doing this the spike will be vertical, straight and not bent nor hanging where it is vulnerable to snap off. If you do this as you see the spike developing, when the flowers open they will be the correct way up. If you wait too long and attempt to tie the spike when the buds are formed they will have oriented themselves to be the right way up depending on the position of the spike before it was tied up.

So as to avoid any nasty shocks on a cold and frosty morning in the event of a failed heater, do make sure that it is serviced regularly.

PART 3
THE ORCHIDS

CHAPTER 15

The Plants for Your Collection

Before you begin to read this part of the book, let me refer you back to the Introduction, which provides a summary of the terminology we shall use. For instance, *Angraecum* Bory: *Angraecum* is the name of the genus and Bory is the name of the man who gave *Angraecum* its name, Col Bory de St Vincent; this is known as the authority. I have not included any biographies about such people, but you could, if you are interested, try the Internet. I have, in addition, used some other terms in describing the plants; these may seem rather technical but I believe that they help to broaden one's knowledge; I have tried to keep them to a minimum and there is a glossary after the Appendices.

ANGRAECUM BORY AND OTHER *ANGRAECUM*-TYPE ORCHIDS

Angraecum (an-gry-kum) is an African genus; it is large, with about 200 species. The name derives from the Malayan word *angurek* or *anggrek* for epiphytic orchids with growth habits similar to those of *Vanda* or *Aerides*, for instance, with aerial roots. It is widely distributed throughout tropical Africa and the Malagasy Republic (Madagascar), but only a quarter of the genus grows in Africa, with the rest mainly on Madagascar, others on the islands in the Indian Ocean, and one species *A. zeylandicum* which grows in Sri Lanka. Other angraecoid orchids requiring the same conditions as *Angraecum* are *Aeranthes*, *Aerides*, *Aerangis*, *Crytopus*, *Cyrtorchis*, *Diaphananthe*, *Jummellia*, *Oeonia*, *Oeoniella* and *Tridactyle*.

The genus was named by Col Bory de St Vincent in 1804 in his *Voyages*. *Angraecum* was one of the first African species to be described; at that time they were all put in the genus *Angraecum*, though many have since been reclassified into other genera. *Angraecum* is a genus of great diversity both in form of foliage and in size.

General Description

Angraecums can be tiny or very large, almost stemless or with a long, sometimes climbing, stem, with thin textured or fleshy leaves, flattened in the usual way: bilaterally or needle-shaped – almost every variation is represented. Flowers are green, white, yellowish or dull orange-salmon, scented in the evening and at night. The lip is unlobed, deeply concave, spurred at the base, although the spur maybe slender or sac-like. Sepals and petals may be similar in size and shape, with the column deeply divided in front.

Culture

Angraecum is an easy genus to grow in the greenhouse, but it is probably not a good plant for indoor

Angraecum sesquipidale *in the wild growing on a tree trunk (left) and in a plastic pot in cultivation (below).* A. sesquipidale *is a plant from Madagascar. Charles Darwin, on seeing the plant, suggested that the pollinator is very specific; he concluded this by observing the long spur of the flower. It can be 30cm (12in) long, and he correctly noted that the pollinator must have an equally long proboscis. He never observed the pollinator (the moth* Xanthopan morgani praedicta*). You can see these spurs clearly in the photograph left.*

culture. Most are intermediate (10–15°C/50– 60°F) for the montane species, to warm (18°C/65°F) for the lowland species. All require humid conditions. The amount of shade needed depends on the natural habitat, with the cooler montane species requiring more than the lowland. The genus does not need a winter rest, but it is wise to reduce watering (keeping them moist only) when the plants are not in active growth. Repotting should be carried out in spring as active growth resumes. Use normal bark-based compost, but adjust the grade to suit the species: coarse for the larger sized plants and medium or fine grade for the smaller plants. The plants may be grown in pots or baskets, particularly the lithophytic species. The smaller epiphytic species are better grown as mounted specimens. *A. distichum* and other smaller species are best grown in small pots with a compost of shredded tree-fern fibre or sphagnum moss.

ANGULOA RUIZ & PAVON: TULIP OR CRADLE ORCHID

There are ten species within the genus *Anguloa* (ang-u-low-a) described by Ruiz and Pavon in 1794 and dedicated to Don Francisco de Angulo (*fl.* 1790), a Spanish naturalist. They are distributed through Colombia, Venezuela, Ecuador and Peru. They require temperatures within the cool/intermediate range. The preferred compost consists of a 2:2:1:1 coarse bark, leaf-mould, charcoal and well-rotted farmyard manure mixture. During repotting remove all dead roots, exhausted bulbs and damaged leaves. The best-known plants of this genus are *A. clowesii*

Angulocaste appoco.

Ansellia africana.

Ansellia gigantia.

and *A. ruckeri.* The common name for these plants arises from the ability of the lip to rock back and forth when tilted; the lip is enclosed by the petals and sepals which do not open fully and thus look a little tulip-like.

ANSELLIA LINDLEY

Ansellia (an-sel-ee-ah) is a small genus, found by John Ansell for whom it is named, having been described by John Lindley in 1844. This genus, although small, has generated much discussion among botanists about how many species belong to it. The consensus seems to suggest that there is only a single species *A. africana*, but there are one or two varieties. *A. africana* is commonly known as the leopard orchid because of its dark spots on a yellow ground. The plant grows in open woodland in hot dry areas, but is also found in wetter forests or woodlands. It is widespread throughout tropical and South Africa and is epiphytic, often growing in the fork of a tree.

General Description

Ansellia have elongated pseudobulbs up to 60cm (23in) long. The leaves are lanceolate and ribbed. The inflorescence emerges from a node at the apex of the pseudobulb; it is branched and may be 80cm (31in) in length.

Culture

Ansellia grows well in a hanging basket, but, because of its size, you will be better using a floral hanging basket. Use normal bark-based compost. It prefers intermediate to warm conditions, and should be watered and fed frequently during active growth, with watering being reduced during the winter in order to give it an almost dry rest. It needs plenty of light and humidity in order to flower well, which it does in spring.

BULBOPHYLLUM THOUARS

The genus (bul-bow-fil-um) was described and named in 1822 by Aubert du Petit Thouars in his monograph *Orchidées des Iles Australes d'Afrique.* The epithet refers to the 'bulb-shaped' leaf, from the Greek *bulbos* (bulb), *phyllum* (leaf), with reference to the leafy pseudobulbs. *Bulbophyllum* is the largest genus within the Orchidaceae with from 1,000 to 1,500 species growing in tropical and subtropical regions around the world. Its size reflects also its diversity. New Guinea is its centre of origin, with an estimated 600 species. Because it is such a large genus, the size of plants within it varies from the very small (whose dimensions can only be discerned by using a magnifying glass; these live on the leaves of other plants) to many large and spectacular ones at the other extreme.

Bulbophyllum lobbii *was considered by John Lindley to be the finest species of this large genus. He named it in 1847 in the* Botanical Register *(sub t 29) after Thomas Lobb, who discovered it in Java while collecting for Veitch.*

General Description

Bulbophyllum may be epiphytic or lithophytic, with the rhizomes being variable from creeping to pendulous and covered by membranous sheaths. The pseudobulbs are stalkless (sessile), usually angular in shape and may be clustered or remote from each other. The leaves are also variable, from having no stalks (petioles) to having petioles, from thin to fleshy or coriaceous. The inflorescence emerges from the base of the pseudobulb and may be erect or pendulous. There may be a single or many flowers; they may be racemes, umbels or spikes.

Culture

Bulbophyllum is a relatively easy genus to grow in the warm to intermediate greenhouse. They are best grown in small, shallow pots, on fibre rafts or in baskets.

BRASSIA R. BROWN

Brassia (bras-ee-ah) was named after William Brass, a botanical illustrator and plant collector who worked for Sir Joseph Banks in Africa. *Brassia* is a genus found in Central and South America, some of the islands of the Caribbean and in southern Florida. Because of the flower shape they have earned the common name of spider orchid.

General Description

The plants form stout, creeping rhizomes and have rather flattish pseudobulbs that have sheathing bracts. The leaves are large, leathery and yet pliable, and there are usually three coming from the end of the pseudobulb. The inflorescence emerges from the base of the pseudobulb and carries a number of flowers depending on the species. These vary in size also and are showy. The flowers are scented and vary in colour from yellow to ivory-white. The petals and sepals are quite long, spreading and very narrow.

Culture

This is a good subject for the cool to intermediate house. *Brassia* is a plant that does not really like to be disturbed and for this reason is best grown in a hanging basket with a good quality, free-draining bark mix. The plant will spread outwards and upwards, with many aerial roots; this is a sign of a healthy plant. Because the plant can grow into a large specimen, the best basket is the floral hanging type. When in active growth they should be liberally watered and fed. Provide the plant with light shade and high temperatures (hang close to the roof). The watering and temperature may be reduced during the winter, but keep the plant just moist to avoid the shrivelling of the pseudobulbs. Resume watering and feeding when new roots and growths are seen. Plants can be propagated by division.

Brassia rex.

CALANTHE R. BROWN

Calanthe (ka-lan-thee), whose name derives from the Greek *kalos* (beautiful) and *anthe* (flower), is a genus of terrestrial orchids with about 150 species. *Calanthe* is found in Africa and Madagascar, throughout South-East Asia and in Australia. The genus is divided into two sections: those with large pseudobulbs that are also deciduous being defined as *Vestitae*; the other section has small, insignificant pseudobulbs, broad, spreading leaves and dense racemes of flowers; these are defined as *Veratrifoliae*. *Calanthe* is an important genus in the history of orchids and their hybridization, when, in the 1850s, the Veitch nursery recorded the first orchid hybrids *C. Dominyi* and *C. Veitchii.*

Culture

Calanthe comprises both deciduous and evergreen species. The deciduous species are the cool growers. The flowers will emerge during winter from their bulbs. The routine for dealing with these is thus: when the pseudobulb has completed its growth it should be dried out and placed in a cool (10°C/50°F), light place. When the foliage has withered, the root activity has ceased and the new bulb has become firm, clean and is covered in an onion-like skin, detach it from the withered pseudobulb. Remove all dead roots. The new bulb can now be potted up in a mixture of leaf-mould, turfy loam, charcoal, finely composted bark and dried farmyard manure. The mix should be well drained. Pot up the bulbs singly using the mixture, but bury only the very base. The temperature should now be raised to about 18°C (64°F) along with the humidity in order to start the new roots and restart growth. A high humidity will promote flowering.

Calanthe vestita.

CATTLEYA LINDL.

The name *Cattleya* (kat-lay-ah, kat-lee-ah) commemorates William Cattley (d. 1832), an English horticulturalist living and working in Barnet, north London; he was the man who first got a cattleya to flower. There are fifty species in the genus and they are epiphytic or lithophytic and distributed through Central and South America. The cattleya has many close relatives and, as such, this makes it one of the classic candidates for hybridization. The genetic make-up of the cattleya is compatible with that of other species such as *Laelia*, *Brassovola*, *Epidendron*, *Broughtonia*, *Diacrium*, *Schomburgkia*, *Sophronitis* and *Leptotes*. Hybridizers have been quick to take advantage of this genetic compatibility and have made many crosses between these plants. Hence a laeliocattleya is a cross between a *Laelia* and a *Cattleya*, or LC for short. This crossing will result in giving the offspring the attributes of the parents, depending on the dominant gene. To illustrate this let us take LC Chit-chat 'tangerine'; this was produced by crossing *Cattleya aurantiaca* and *Laelia* Coronet and has the smaller, more delicate flower of the *Laelia* rather than the larger *Cattleya* type. From here the crossing does tend to get complicated with three- and four-way crosses. Brassolaeliocattleya is a cross between *Brassovola* and Laeliocattleya. Potinaria is a four-ways or quadrigeneric cross between *Brassovola* × *Cattleya* × *Laelia* × *Sophronitis*. Likewise, other genera have produced many intergeneric hybrids, and each has been given a strange-sounding name.

General Description

Cattleya has more or less thickened pseudobulbs, with either one or two leaves which are thick, fleshy and leathery (coriaceous). The inflorescence emerges from the apex of the pseudobulb on completion of growth. The number of flowers produced varies, sometimes several, sometimes only one. An important feature which aids identification is the number of leaves. Unofoliate species produce a single leaf and bifoliate produce two. A typical unifoliate has several sturdy, upright, green growths. Each will be about 20cm (8in) tall. The pseudobulbs are more or less parallel to each other, usually wider in the middle than at the ends. The bulbs are terminated by a single, large leaf, which may be 30cm (12in) long. The leaf will be very stiff and will snap if you try to bend it. The bifoliate bulb, on the other hand, terminates with two leaves. These are sometimes known as cluster types because they usually produce several flowers from the one bulb, but there are, of course, the exceptions which produce single flowers. These bulbs differ from the unifoliates' by being fatter, taller, shorter or rounder and some are quite diminutive. *Cattleya* is one of those groups of orchids that you either love or hate. The species may have small, delicate flowers or larger ones with curled edges to the petals. The hybrids, on the other hand, may be very large and flamboyant.

Culture

Cattleya is a plant for the intermediate section (12–15°C/54–60°F). They like good light and humidity and may be grown either in pots or baskets. If you use pots, then all-plastic pots should be weighted with something fairly heavy because cattleyas can grow to be quite large and heavy. I grow

Cattleya *'new dawn'*.

BELOW: Cattleya.

ABOVE: Cattleya *hybrid.*

Cattleya *hybrid.*

Cattleya *hybrid.*

Cattleya *hybrid.*

Cattleya *hybrid.*

Cattleya *hybrid.*

many of my cattleyas in floral hanging baskets. This serves cattleyas well because it allows good drainage and, with the use of an automatic watering system, you will be able to give your plants regular watering and feeding. The basket can also be hung close to the roof, which will afford better light. The compost should be a coarse, open, bark mix (or cork granules).

The annual routine for cattleyas should begin when the new growth is seen in spring. The new growth will be seen emerging from the base of the previous year's pseudobulb. As it extends, new root

ABOVE: Cattleya *hybrid.*

RIGHT: Cattleya *hybrid.*

growth will also begin. You must be careful with watering at this time because you may easily cause the rotting of the new growth. As the growth extends and the roots elongate you may begin to water, but carefully at first. When the roots are growing well you may increase watering and also begin to feed. During the summer, watering and feeding may be done quite heavily because the plant has to produce much growth in a relatively short time. The atmosphere around your cattleyas should be humid with plenty of air movement (a 'buoyant atmosphere').

CHYSIS LINDL.

The name *Chysis* (kye-sis) derives from the Greek *kysis*, meaning melting, a reference to the fused pollinia occurring in self-fertilizing forms. There are six species within the genus, all of which are epiphytic. It is distributed from Mexico to Peru.

General Description

Chysis has rather stout, club-shaped pseudobulbs, with the plant forming a clump and being slightly pendulous. The leaves are apical and alternate along the upper part of the pseudobulb; they are broad-lanceolate, arching, plicate or ribbed, either thin textured or slightly fleshy. *Chysis* is a deciduous plant with the leaves falling after one season, that is, they will be held until the new bulb has developed. The inflorescence emerges from the base of the new bulb and arches slightly, bearing rather fleshy, fragrant flowers.

Culture

Chysis is best grown in a basket where it can develop undisturbed for as long as possible. It should be placed in a light position, with dappled shade in intermediate temperature conditions. During the growing season supply copious amounts of water and feed every two weeks. When the bulbs are complete, reduce watering to a minimum and stop feeding and place the plants in cooler conditions. The new growth and the flowers emerge almost simultaneously; you should gradually increase watering and the temperature during the flowering period.

Chysis are autogamous, which means that they are self-fertile and therefore will develop seed pods quite readily; but, unless you intend to try and germinate them, it is as well to remove the inflorescence when the flowers are over. The plant will then put all its energy into producing strong pseudobulbs, instead of seeds.

COELOGYNE LINDL.

The genus name derives from the Greek *koilos*, hollow and *gyne*, female, referring to the deep stigmatic cavity. The pronunciation of the name from this interpretation should possibly be *koi-lo-GUY-nee*, but through common usage it is pronounced either *see-lo-GUY nee* or *see-LODGE-eh-nee*. *Coelogyne* is a large, diverse genus with about 190 species from South-East Asia.

Culture

There are specimens growing in all temperature ranges because *Coelogyne* in the wild may be found from sea level up to 2,900m (9,500ft). This makes it difficult to generalize cultural information about it. However, most of the *Coelogyne* will do well in cool to intermediate conditions; they like plenty of light, but avoid direct sun. If you give them too much shade they tend to develop larger leaves at the expense of flowers. The warm growers like plenty of water when in growth, but, at the end of the growing season, you should reduce the watering to almost nil – just enough to prevent excessive shrinkage of the bulbs. The growth habit of many *Coelogyne* is to creep along on a rhizome, and some tend to extend vertically. The distance between bulbs also makes it difficult to confine them in a pot. Placing them in seed trays or fastening them on to a compost-filled sleeve (*see* Chapter 12) is good practice. Those that form a more compact clump may be placed in a hanging basket. The warmer growing species also tend to be the larger growing types; *C. asperata*, for instance, has leaves almost 1m (3ft 3in) long. These like high humidity, but if it is low they tend to get brown spots on their leaves.

Coelogyne ovalis.

Coelogyne *mem. William Micholitz.*

Coelogyne fimbriata.

Resting

I used to give mine a dry rest in winter, which resulted in the shrivelling of the pseudobulbs. The bulbs in many cases failed to swell again when watering was resumed. Recently I read that in the wild they experience a climate that produces mists during the morning, with 90 per cent humidity. These conditions are year-long, even in the dry season. I would suggest therefore that during the rest period they should receive a spray during the morning in order to simulate those conditions. An occasional light watering could also be given if you feel that the pseudobulbs are shrivelling too much. It was also suggested that, while the rainfall may be low during the dry season, the plants had a soaking every morning with the dew.

Inflorescences

Many species of *Coelogyne* have pendulous inflorescences, which should hang down. Some may have a tendency not to grow long enough to get over the side of the pot. Keep an eye open for the development of the inflorescence and carefully train it over the side of the pot, otherwise it will bury itself in compost and rot. A piece of thin, pliable plastic is useful for this job.

CYMBIDIUM SWARTZ

Olaf Swartz, a Swedish botanist, described *Cymbidium* (sim-bid-ee-um) in 1799; the name derives from the Greek *kymbes*, boat, referring to the shape of the lip. There are about seventy species within the genus, distributed around South-East Asia and into northern Australia. They are a popular orchid and many thousands of hybrids have been produced. Cymbidium over recent years has lost some of its popularity, because it can grow into a very large plant; a well-grown, standard cymbidium may easily fill a space of 1sq m (11sq ft) with its spread of leaves. However, smaller versions are now available, the miniatures, and these are excellent for the home. Standard cymbidiums, despite their size, are still worth growing, but they do need careful attention to their cultural needs.

ABOVE: Coelogyne pandorata.

RIGHT: Coelogyne massangeana.

BELOW: Coelogyne *hybrid*, C. cristata × C. massangeana.

Culture

These are mainly cool-growing orchids and require temperatures between 8° and 10°C minimum in winter (about 50°F). They do not like high temperatures, even in summer, which makes them ideal for outdoor culture in northern Europe. In southern Europe, the Canary Islands or Madeira they could remain outdoors all year round with

LEFT: Cymbidium *hybrid.*

ABOVE: Cymbidium *hybrid.*

BELOW: Cymbidium *hybrid.*

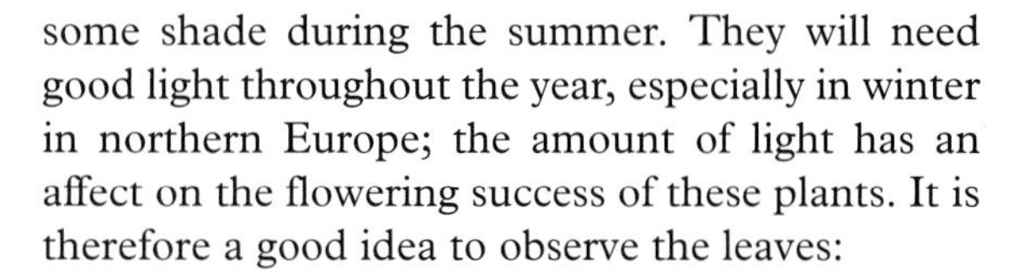

some shade during the summer. They will need good light throughout the year, especially in winter in northern Europe; the amount of light has an affect on the flowering success of these plants. It is therefore a good idea to observe the leaves:

- soft and dark green mean too little light;
- light green, firm and a satisfactory texture mean that the lighting is adequate;

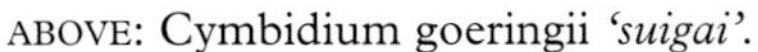

ABOVE: Cymbidium goeringii *'suigai'*.

ABOVE RIGHT: Cymbidium goeringii uzengomachi.

RIGHT: Cymbidium *hybrid.*

- leaf ends black or red mean too much sun, and also a sign of drought.

Getting the conditions right is crucial for this species to flower well, but it is, nevertheless, an easy orchid to grow. So how do we do this?

Pot and Compost

The pot, as with all orchids, should not be too large; over-potting leads to an over-wet compost and a dead orchid. The pot may be plastic or terracotta. The compost has to be well-drained; although some of these plants are terrestrial they are treated as semi-epiphytic and, as such, traditional, bark-based composts are used.

Watering and Feeding

Watering should be carried out all year round, with an increase during the summer when the plants are in active growth. Cymbidiums are hungry plants and feed should therefore be given at half the

Cymbidium *hybrids.*

recommended dosage every fortnight throughout the growing season. Use a high nitrogen feed at the start of the growing season for a few weeks to give them a boost, then use a balanced feed through the summer; you should change to a high potassium feed through the autumn. No feed should be given during the winter (*see also* Chapter 8).

Temperature

Cymbidiums require a cool environment. Many people buy cymbidiums as houseplants and tend to keep them too warm. As a result, they get lovely green foliage but no flowers. The plants themselves are happy in this environment, but in the wild they do suffer some 'hardship', the trigger for flowering. Plants produce flowers in order that they may make seed to continue the species. If the conditions are good, then there is no need to exert energy in producing seed. So what temperature should they have? As a winter day minimum this should be around 10°C (50°F); this can fall to 8°C (46°F) with no worries. During the summer cymbidiums may be put outdoors in northern Europe; but they should be kept in a position where they receive dappled shade and where they are not in a draught. They may remain outdoors until early autumn, or at least until the night temperature falls to 6°C (43°F); the absolute minimum is 4°C (40°F).

Care
Repot cymbidiums every 18 months to two years in well-drained compost. As the flower spike grows, insert a green split cane next to the spike and loosely tie it to the cane with twist tie wire. This will not only support the spike but will also keep it straight (the better for showing). You can secure the ties more firmly when the spike is fully grown. The cane need only be as high as the lowest flower bud. Tidy up the wire by snipping it clean near to the twist.

Propagation
Cymbidiums may be propagated easily, first by division which is done at the same time as repotting, and secondly from leafless back-bulbs (*see* Chapter 10).

DENDROBIUM SWARTZ

The genus *Dendrobium* (den-droe-be-um) is another of the larger orchid families, with about 1,400 species (140 in New Guinea alone), and more hybrids than you might care to think about.

General Description

The name derives from the Greek *dendros*, tree and *bios*, life, referring to their epiphytic habit. All dendrobiums are epiphytes or lithophytes and are found in India, South-East Asia, China, Japan and through all the Pacific islands into Australia and New Zealand. Dendrobiums are also very diverse, as one would expect from the number of species present. They are to be found from sea level – the warm growing species, up into the foothills of the Himalayas – the cool growing species. Their diversity also encompasses their size – from 1cm or so, to more than 3m (10ft) tall, and their shape – with long, slender, pendulous canes, or with fleshy, terete, flattened, succulent leaves. Dendrobiums also inhabit all temperature zones so it is difficult to generalize when speaking of their cultural needs. I think it best to deal with the common types, and the most common are the nobile (no-bee-lay) or upright-canes forms. Dendrobiums may be deciduous or at least semi-deciduous; *Dendrobium nobile* may or may not shed all its leaves, but they certainly drop some so do not worry if this happens.

Culture

There are four important features to follow if you are to succeed with this genus.

Watering: Amount and Frequency
Dendrobiums inhabit regions which experience seasons that are wet and dry, and these generally correspond with our winter and summer. During the winter they need not be watered, but they do need to be in a humid atmosphere or have some dampness around their roots to prevent the shrivelling of the bulbs; this is the dormant or rest period. At this time many will have shed their leaves from that year's growth and will survive leafless until new growth forms in the following season. Likewise, the roots are usually annual and new roots will form along with new growth each year. As the new growth develops and the roots extend, watering should begin carefully. This is gradually increased as the

Group of dendrobiums on the show bench.

ABOVE LEFT: Dendrobium montrose.

ABOVE: Dendrobium chrysotorum.

Dendrobium nobile.

A Dendrobium *from Singapore.*

BELOW: Dendrobium densiflora.

BELOW RIGHT: Dendrobium *Golden Crescent.*

plants grow and they can be given copious amounts during the summer. Feeding can be done at every or every other watering during summer and gradually eased off from late summer into autumn as growth ceases. The maintaining of a humid atmosphere is essential and so damping down or the use of automisting apparatus in the greenhouse is necessary.

Temperature: by Night and Day
Most species need some additional heating; *D. nobile* is cool growing and 10°C (50°F) is satisfactory. A daytime rise in temperature of 5°C (37°F) is necessary throughout the year, and at least 10° to 15°C (18° to 27°F) rise during summer; but these increases should not be a problem even in winter if the greenhouse is sited in the best position.

Light
This is especially important during the winter and, conversely, so is shade in the summer months. In northern Europe no shading will be needed from about October to March. Shading will, however, be needed during the height of the summer – June to August. When the day is not hot and sunny, the shading can be drawn back, so its easy movement should be considered. During spring and autumn the shading will also have to be carefully controlled because the greenhouse may become too hot at these times; too high a temperature at the wrong time, when new growth is forming, may stunt growth and scorch leaves.

Fresh Air
This is associated with shading and the maintenance of a buoyant atmosphere. Vents in the roof and sides of a greenhouse may be used. Electric oscillating fans are also useful for helping to keep leaves cool (*see* Chapter 8).

Propagation

Dendrobiums frequently produce keikis which can be separated from the parent plant and potted on separately. During repotting, a leafless backbulb can be removed and laid in a seed tray on a bed of damp moss and covered. Keep this in a light place but out of direct sun. New growths will come from the adventitious buds at the nodes.

DRACULA LUER

The epithet refers to the rather strange and bizarre flowers of some species (from Latin *Dracula*, little dragon). There are about a hundred species in the genus; all are tufted epiphytic or lithophytic. Originally they were included in the *Masdevallia* but were distinguished by their pendulous flowers. They are to be found in the wild through Central America, Colombia, Ecuador and Peru.

Dracula.

Culture

They require a buoyant, shady, humid atmosphere of intermediate conditions (14°C/57°F) and require frequent mistings. They should be grown in teak hanging baskets that allow them plenty of room to spread as they produce offsets. In many species the older leaf tips discolour and die back – a problem observed in the wild and seldom affecting the health of the plant.

EPIDENDRUM LINDL. (ALSO *ENCYCLIA* HOOKER)

The name comes from the Greek *epi*, upon and *dendron*, tree, and refers to the epiphytic habit of the genus. It is interesting to note that, from their discovery in the early 1700s, all epiphytes were known as *Epidendrum* (eh-pi-den-drum). There are 500 species, originating from Mexico, through Central into South America and some of the Caribbean islands. This is another of the very diverse genera, with plants suitable for the cool, intermediate and warm greenhouse. Epidendrums are easy plants to grow and, because of the diversity of their growth habit and form, they make interesting additions to a mixed collection. They could even become a speciality subject.

Culture

They need fairly good light (*E. ibaguense* prefers full sun), but generally the normal shading precautions should be taken. The temperature needs of the epidendrums should be considered in relation to the species. Generally, this genus is divided into those with pseudobulbs and those with canes – which can be divided further into the tall types and the short cane types. The *pseudobulb types* can be treated as

Epidendrum.

OPPOSITE PAGE:
Epidendrum.

THIS PAGE:
Epidendrum.

are *Laelia* species. They can be potted tightly in open, bark-based compost and be grown in cool to intermediate conditions. They need plenty of light and a cool, dry rest and are propagated by division. The *tall-growing types*, such as *E. ibaguence*, can reach several metres in length and be trained along the length of the greenhouse. This species is quite amenable as to temperature and will grow in cool to frost-free sunny houses or intermediate greenhouses. It has either red or yellow flowers which it produces at almost any time of the year. You will need to provide a foothold for it in a medium-sized pot containing a mixture of bark and well-rotted farmyard manure. Syringe and foliar feed the foliage regularly as this encourages good flowering. Propagate via plantlets and offshoots. The *shorter-caned types* need intermediate conditions, high humidity with dappled shade and a semi-dry rest and are propagated by division. For all species use a balanced feed at half strength.

LAELIA LINDL.

The genus was named in reference to *Laelia*, one of the vestal virgins of Rome. It has about seventy species that are all either epiphytic or lithophytic. *Laelia* (lay-lee-a) is closely allied to *Cattleya*, from which association many hybrids have been created. The genus is distributed through Central and South America and the West Indies.

Culture

This is similar to the handling of *Cattleya*, and can be grown in the intermediate house or in a sunny, humid position indoors. *Laelia* is divided into four vegetative-based groups that have differing cultural needs.

Group I
This comprises large, showy species and includes *L. crispa*, *L. purpurata* and *L. tenebrosa*; they should be grown as for for *Cattleya* types.

Group II
As Group I, but these are slightly squatter plants with slender racemes of magenta flowers. Groups I and II should be potted in a very open compost of large-grade bark or cork granules, or mounted on rafts. When in full growth, water well but a drier, cooler autumn rest will encourage flower development. They should flower in winter. They are generally cool-growing species (7°C/45°F) but should also be given as much sunlight as possible.

Laelia.

BELOW LEFT: Laelia.

BELOW: Laelia.

Group III

L. harpophylla is typical of the group and has a habit described as 'willowy', with slender bulbs and leaves. The group does better in a denser compost, along with high humidity and dappled shade. During the semi-dry rest period only enough water should be given to prevent the shrivelling of the pseudobulbs.

Group IV

This is composed of semi-dwarf plants with broad leaves and rounded bulbs. This group does well in compost similar to that appropriate to Group III, with additional sphagnum or rockwool and in very small pots or baskets. This group grows in intermediate conditions in full sunlight, with plenty of water during active growth but followed by a cooler, dry rest. During the rest period careful watering should be done to prevent the shrivelling of the bulbs and the roots from dying.

LYCASTE LINDL.

This genus was named to honour Lycaste, the daughter of King Priam of Troy. There are thirty-five species within the genus. They grow as epiphytes, terrestrials or lithophytes, and were first described in 1843 by John Lindley. They are distributed through Central America and northern South America to Peru. *Lycaste* (lye-kass-tee) is split into two groups, depending on whether or not they lose their leaves in winter or keep them. The watering regime differs accordingly.

Culture

In their natural environment the conditions will vary, and so you may need to consider the species in your collection carefully and respond accordingly. They need as much light as you can give them, but careful shading is required. The objective with watering is to produce a large, solid pseudobulb during the summer months and so water copiously during active growth. In autumn watering should be eased off and the plant given a fairly dry rest with only enough water to prevent the bulbs from shrivelling. Use a balanced feed once a fortnight. The compost for these plants should be a mixture of bark, charcoal, sphagnum and leaf mould.

Lycaste.

Lycaste skineri.

BELOW: Lycaste.

MASDEVALLIA RUIZ AND PAVON

The genus was named in honour of the Spanish botanist and physician Jose Masdeval (d. 1801). It comprises 350 species of generally small, evergreen plants that grow epiphytically, but sometimes lithophytically, generally forming clumps. The genus is distributed throughout Central and South America in the cloud forests areas. *Masdevallia* (maz-de-val-lee-a) has some of the more unusual flowers within the Orchidaceae.

Culture

In the wild they tend to grow at altitude and are therefore cool growers, with a minimum temperature of 5°C (40°F) in winter, but care should be taken not to allow the daytime temperature to get above 25°C (77°F) during the summer. All like a diurnal (day–night) fluctuation in temperature of at least 10°C (18°F). If these plants are placed in too hot a position you will get only attractive green plants but no flowers. Growth may even deteriorate. Being cool growers, these plants need a buoyant, humid, cool

Masdevallia.

Masdevallia.

environment. To achieve this circulation, fans should be incorporated in the greenhouse. Plenty of air movement should be ensured since the plants are susceptible to damping off (a fungal infection). Always make certain that you can see the leaves moving gently in the breeze; if not, install extra small fans to move the air in the dead spots. It is suggested that you should water from the base by standing the pots on wet gravel and allowing the roots to grow and search for water, as they would in the wild. It is usually good horticultural practice to get plants to develop an extensive root system by watering from the bottom. They all like to be sprayed regularly. The compost usually consists of a mixture of fine bark, charcoal and sphagnum or coir fibre and sphagnum moss in clay pots with good drainage. Good light should be provided, but care should be taken to provide light without allowing the temperature to rise above the maximum. Excessive shading will keep the house cool but it will also keep the light level down. By using aluminium shade material giving 50 per cent shade or normal green shade cloth, fitted to provide space between the glass and the cloth, good results should be achieved (*see* Chapter 6).

MAXILLARIA RUIZ AND PAVON

Maxillaria (max-il-lair-ee-a) is a genus of 600 species. The epithet refers to the similarity of the lip to the jaw, from the Latin *maxilla*. It is distributed through tropical America, from Mexico to Brazil, and the West Indies. The plants are generally epiphytic, of varying size and structure, either having pseudobulbs or virtually none. If there are pseudobulbs, they are tightly clustered, usually sheathed,

Maxillaria.

and some may be leaf bearing. The pseudobulbs are single leaved. The inflorescence is single flowered and many are scented.

Culture

Maxillaria are cool to intermediate growing. The compost should be open and well drained for pot-grown specimens. *Maxillaria* may also be mounted on rafts. When in active growth they may be watered and fed regularly, at other times water lightly and withhold feed. They need be given only a short rest when growth is complete.

MILTONIA LINDL.

Miltonia was named in honour of the Earl Fitzwilliam, Viscount Milton (1786–1857), a landowner and orchid enthusiast. The genus is made up of about twenty species distributed from Panama

Miltonia.

and Costa Rica to Peru and eastern Brazil. *Miltonia* is an epiphytic plant with short, rather inconspicuous pseudobulbs that are also compressed, at the apex they bear two leaves and the base is sheathed.

Culture

All species like plenty of water and moderate shade when in active growth, with the watering being reduced when the pseudobulbs are fully grown. Those species that have clusters of pseudobulbs are best grown in pots and those with a creeping habit in shallow trays.

MILTONIOPSIS GODEFROY-LEBEUF

The name is derived from its similarity to *Miltonia*, with the suffix *opsis* from the Greek meaning resemblance. *Miltoniopsis* is sometimes known as the pansy orchid because the flat face of its flower is pansy-like. There are five species in the genus of this epiphytic plant, distributed through Costa Rica, Panama, Venezuela, Ecuador and Colombia. They have short rhizomes with clustered pseudobulbs, each having a solitary leaf.

Culture

These plants are best grown in relatively small pots. They should be given good shade and humidity and watered all year round, with more being given when they are in active growth.

ODONTOGLOSSUM HUMBOLDT, BONPLAND & KUNTH

In 1815 Alexander von Humboldt, Aimé Bonpland and Carl Sigismund Kunth first described the genus *Odontoglossum*. The name derives from the Greek *odontos*, tooth and *glossa*, tongue, referring to the tooth-like processes of the lip. There are some sixty species within the genus, either epiphytic or lithophytic. The pseudobulbs are compressed, usually ovoid, on a short rhizome which creeps over the substrate surface. At the apex of the bulb there are from one to three leaves which are coriaceous or fleshy and vary in shape. This is a genus that has been used

Odontoglossum.

to hybridize with allied genera such as *Miltonia*, *Brassia*, *Oncidium*, *Osmoglossum* and *Rossioglossum*.

Culture

Odontoglossum is a cool-house plant where a light, humid buoyant atmosphere is required. Some shade should be given during the summer. The roots of *Odontoglossum* are fine and thus a fine grade of bark-based compost is recommended. Water and spray frequently when in full growth, but watering should be eased off during winter; they should not be sprayed at this time either. Give a balanced feed when in active growth only. It is wise to water without fertilizer on every third application in order to flush out of the compost any excess of salts. The flower spikes can be trained by tying them to split canes with twist-tie wire. *Odontoglossums* may produce more than one spike on a single plant. The production of flowers has a weakening effect by using up a great deal of the energy reserves. If you leave a plant with multiple spikes it may have such a detrimental effect on the plant that it may never recover. It is advisable therefore to remove the flower spikes and use them in an arrangement with other cut flowers, or allow only one spike to develop on any one plant. Propagation is by division, which is carried out when repotting, or by using back-bulbs, but there must be a clump of at least three bulbs. These must be clean and free from pests and disease. They can be placed in a pot of damp compost in a propagator and covered with a lid with the vents open in order to maintain a fresh atmosphere.

Odontoglossum.

ABOVE: Odontoglossum.

ABOVE RIGHT: Odontoglossum.

Odontoglossum *hybrid*.

OPPOSITE PAGE:
Oncidium.

ONCIDIUM SWARTZ

The genus name derives from the Greek *onkos*, meaning mass or body, referring to the fleshy, warty calli on the lip of many species. Olaf Swartz classified the genus in 1800. It is a large genus of 450 species of epiphytic, lithophytic or terrestrial plants, distributed throughout sub-tropical and tropical America. The genus is allied to *Odontoglossum*, *Brassia*, *Miltonia* and *Psychopsis*. As with many large genera, their vegetative forms and their habitats are equally diverse. *Oncidium* are best recognized by their long, slender, branched, arching sprays of flowers that are shades of brown and yellow.

Culture

Oncidium frequents cool to intermediate conditions; they are best grown where they can be given plenty of light so that flower development will not be inhibited. The watering regime needs to be carefully controlled since they do not like to be too wet

ABOVE: Oncidium papilio.

Oncidium.

LEFT: Oncidium.

BELOW LEFT: Paphiopedilum.

at the roots. The compost therefore should remain moist yet be freely draining. The smaller species with pronounced pseudobulbs and relatively soft growth require dappled sunlight and a buoyant humid environment in the cool section. They will require plenty of water during active growth but this should be reduced during the dormant period to just enough to prevent the shrivelling of the bulbs. The compost recommended is a fine to medium grade, bark-based mix. The plants may be grown in pots or baskets.

Another group of *Oncidium* lacks pseudobulbs; they have large, leathery leaves and are sometime known as 'mules' ears'. These are best grown in either baskets or mounted on bark. They should be placed in a position where they can receive the maximum light and humidity throughout the year. Their watering requirement is not so great as that of the first group, but they tend to favour a warmer, steamier situation. Some species produce very long inflorescences and will need to be trained around a wire support if they are not to hit the ceiling.

PAPHIOPEDILUM PFITZ

This genus is instantly recognized by most people, whether orchid growers or not, as the lady's slipper orchid. This is because of the distinctive shape of the lip forming a pocket that resembles the end of a slipper. *Paphiopedilum* is a member of the Cypripedioideae, of which there are four related genera: *Cypripedium*, which originates from the temperate zones of the northern hemisphere; *Phragmipedium*, which comes from South America; *Selenipedium*, also from South America; and *Paphiopedilum*, which originates from the Far East. The name *Paphiopedilum* comes from that of the Greek island of Paphos, where there is a temple to Aphrodite, and *pedilon*, meaning slipper hence Venus's slipper, changed to lady's slipper at some time. Similarly, *Cypripedium* comes from the name Cyprus, another island sacred to Venus.

Paphiopedilum.

Paphiopedilum.

OPPOSITE PAGE:
TOP: Paphiopedilum.

BOTTOM LEFT: Paphiopedilum.

BOTTOM RIGHT: Paphiopedilum.

Culture

These plants are terrestrial and thus the compost must not be allowed to dry out or allowed to become waterlogged. Compost made up of bark, sphagnum and/or coir, perlite and charcoal is suitable for these plants. The compost should be freely draining but retain moisture without becoming too wet. Plants should be watered all year round and a balanced fertilizer used during summer. This may be applied more frequently if foliar feeding is carried out. There should be good humidity (60–70 per cent in summer and 50 in winter). 'Paphs' are forest plants and so do not need strong light; too much will cause the leaves to yellow or turn a pale green. The leaf colour should be a healthy, dark green. There should be good air circulation around the greenhouse to maintain a buoyant atmosphere. There are two forms of Paphs, one with wholly green leaves and one with pleasingly mottled leaves. The former are cool growers, with the latter requiring warmer conditions. The temperature should have a rise and fall with day and night. The cool growers like 10–13°C (50–55°F) minimum night temperature with a rise during the day of at least 5°C (9°F).

Propagation

This is done by division of the clump; but it should be carried out with a word of caution – any clump must have at least three or four growths because many are shy to flower until they have multiple growths.

PHALAENOPSIS BLUME

The genus *Phalaenopsis* derives its name from the Greek *phalaina*, meaning moth, and *opsis*, meaning appearance, hence the common name of moth orchid. They are popular as houseplants because the flowers remain in good condition for long periods. There are some sixty species in the genus, originating in Asia from north-east India, Burma and the Philippines to Indonesia, Papua New Guinea and Australia. They are all epiphytic plants for the intermediate to warm greenhouse. It is a genus that has

Phalaenopsis.

Phalaenopsis.

BELOW: Phalaenopsis.

been well hybridized and many thousands of both intra- and intergeneric hybrids have been made.

General Description

The modern hybrid *Phalaenopsis* is rather different from its species cousin. It is characterized by having much rounder petals and sepals which overlap, giving it an almost circular appearance. The species tend to have smaller flowers with the petals and sepals being narrower and separate from one another. The leaves are usually green but some have mottled leaves; a healthy plant will have from two to six leaves that are arranged in two opposite ranks and are ovoid in shape.

Culture

Phalaenopsis are plants for the warm house. In the wild the temperature seldom falls below 24–25°C (75–77°F) but they adapt well to temperatures slightly lower than these; a winter minimum night temperature of 18–20°C (64–68°F) would be satisfactory. An adult plant will however tolerate a drop to a winter night temperature of 15°C (59°F). *Phalaenopsis* will suffer badly if they are kept too wet for too long, their roots will rot and you will lose the plant. Give it a good soaking and allow it to almost dry out completely and then water again. Similarly,

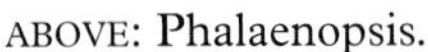

ABOVE: Phalaenopsis.

ABOVE RIGHT: Phalaenopsis.

RIGHT: Phalaenopsis.

do not allow *Phalaenopsis* to dry and remain dry for too long as they do not have pseudobulbs and therefore are not able to withstand long droughts. In the wild they experience high humidity, which means that they never dry completely. When watering, do not allow water to hold in the 'vase' formed by the leaves; this will result in stem rot, especially at low temperatures. Mop up any water with a piece of kitchen paper. The compost should be an open, and well drained yet moisture-retentive mixture. Traditionally bark was used with the addition of moss; a

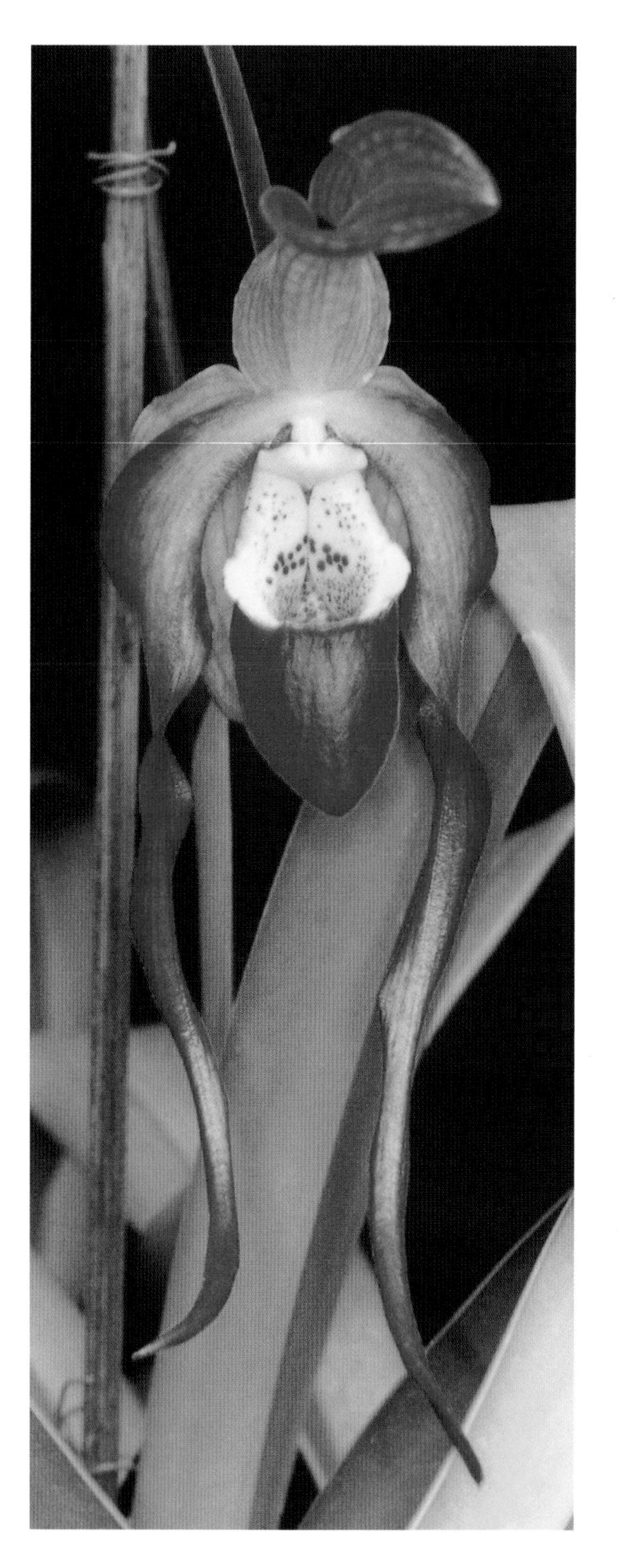

modern alternative is a mixture of lump peat and coir fibre, sometimes with horticultural foam pieces.

Phalaenopsis do not want to be grown in full sun; they will need moderate shade whether in the greenhouse or indoors. If you grow them indoors they are best on an east-facing window sill with shading provided by net curtains. You can allow them more sun in winter since it is less intense and they will not suffer.

If *Phalaenopsis* are growing well they tend to develop roots outside the pot. Do not worry about this and do not try to put them back into the pot. They will simply snap and it is not necessary; keep them sprayed and the plant will be well. When the next repotting session takes place these roots may be put into the pot. *Phalaenopsis* are monopodial; during the growth cycle the lower leaf will discolour and die off, but at the same time a new leaf will appear from the top. They never grow tall, but the leaves may have a spread of up to 30cm (12in). The flower spike, however, can grow very tall, which is the reason for staking it as it grows.

PHRAGMIPEDIUM ROLFE

The name derives from the Greek *phragma*, meaning partition and *pedilon*, meaning slipper, referring to the trilocular ovary and the slipper-like lip. There are about twenty species in this terrestrial, lithophytic or epiphytic genus originating from Central and South America.

General Description

Phragmipedium has a sympodial growth habit with short stems and a fibrous root system, and has tufted fans of from six to eight leaves that are dark green and coriaceous. Some species may have very long leaves up to 90cm (3ft). The inflorescence is erect, axillary, with a many-flowered raceme. Flowers are large and showy, with up to fifteen blooms.

Phragmipedium.

Phragmipedium.

The dorsal sepal is free and lateral sepals unite for the full length into a synsepalum. Petals are free spreading. In *P. caudatum* the lateral petals are elongated and twisted.

Culture

Treat as for warm growing species of *Paphiopedilum*.

PLEUROTHALLIS R. BROWN

The name is derived from the Greek *pleuron*, rib and *thallos*, stem, and refers to the rib-like stems of many species. There are in excess of 1,000 species, making up between 12 and 14 per cent of the orchid kingdom. They are a diverse genus, ranging widely throughout tropical America, between the latitudes formed by the tropics of Cancer and Capricorn. They are to be found from below 500m (1,640ft) up to 3,200m (10,500ft) and, as such, their temperature requirements vary from cool to intermediate. The Pleurothallidinae includes *Pleurothallis* and *Masdevallia*.

The flowering period may be at any time of the year and some will flower continually. Many will flower more than once, sometimes two or three times a year, and many flower in winter – December through to February in the northern hemisphere. The scent of some is pleasant, while others, because they attract carrion flies for pollination, have a rather unpleasant smell.

Culture

The *Pleurothallis* are generally intermediate growers and need 15°C (60°F), but will tolerate temperatures down to 10°C (50°F) in winter. All of them like a day–night fluctuation in temperature, with a

Pleurothallis.

Pleurothallis.

BELOW LEFT: Pleurothallis.

BELOW: Pleurothallis.

daytime rise of at least 10°C (18°F). There should also be high humidity with a buoyant atmosphere. It is a good idea to have plenty of fans to create good air circulation and to ensure that there are no pockets of still air because these may cause serious fungal problems. Watering should be regular throughout the year and the plants should never be allowed to dry out (they do not have pseudobulbs that would enable them to store water); they also benefit from regular spraying. Mounted plants will need daily spraying, possibly more often during the summer. The compost used is made up of coir fibre and sphagnum moss, in a ratio of 5:1. Do not forget to soak the coir prior before use (*see* Chapter 13).

STANHOPEA FROST EX HOOKER

The genus *Stanhopea* was named in honour of the Earl of Stanhope, President of the London Medico-Botanical Society between 1829 and 1837. It is a genus of some fifty-five species from Mexico, through Central America and into Brazil. They are epiphytic plants and occasionally lithophytic. They are allied to *Coryanthes* and *Gongora*.

ABOVE: Pleurothallis.

Stanhopea.

Stanhopea.

General Description

Large pseudobulbs are produced on short rhizomes, with large elliptic to oblong-lanceolate leaves which may be 50cm (20in) in length. The inflorescences emerge in a downward direction, producing a raceme of weird-looking, highly scented, short-lived flowers. Even though individual flowers may be short-lived, they do open in succession, thereby extending the flowering period.

Culture

Stanhopea are best grown in a floral hanging basket because of the downward growth of the inflorescence. One disadvantage with using wire hanging baskets is that new growths tend to appear between the wires and so make it impossible to remove them if you need to divide or replace the compost. I have therefore begun to grow some of mine as a natural clump that I suspend by using stiff wire formed into a hook.

The compost is usually bark-based with the addition of sphagnum. Dolomitic lime may be included at a rate of 3g/ltr. The compost should drain freely but retain moisture. I have set my *Stanhopea* plants up to include auto-watering and feeding. By doing this, the bulbs have increased in size from what they were when I watered them manually. They are subjects for the cool to intermediate house; in the wild they are to be found at altitudes up to 3,000m (9,800ft). They also need a fairly high humidity, but with a buoyant atmosphere. Many people are put off this genus either because of their dimensions or the powerful scent they produce, but one in a collection is worthwhile for the sheer weird-exotic appearance of the flowers.

Stanhopea will grow quite happily for many years undisturbed. They are propagated by division at repotting time.

VANDA JONES AND OTHER VANDACEOUS ORCHIDS

The name *Vanda* comes from the Sanskrit word describing the plant we know today as *Vanda tesselata*, from Bengal, Sri Lanka and Burma. *Vanda* was described in 1795 by Sir W. Jones. There are thirty-five species of this monopodial epiphyte, distributed throughout South-East Asia from India through Malaysia, the Philippines, Papua New Guinea and into northern Australia. Probably the best known of the genus is *V. coerulea*, the blue orchid.

General Description

Some plants are suitable for the warm section and some for the intermediate to cool section. *V. coerulea* and, generally, those plants with flattened leaves, are suited to the intermediate to cool section. Those *Vanda* with terete (rounded) leaves are for the warm section. Many will adapt to the intermediate section, which brings in many more species for cultivation.

Other vandaceous plants treated as for *Vanda* include: *Ascocentrum*, *Euanthe*, *Neofinetia*, *Renanthe*, *Rhinerrhiza*, *Rhynchostylis*, *Papilionanthe* and *Vandopsis*.

Culture

All *Vanda* are monopodial and true epiphytes. Their roots freely hang in the air and so a humid

Vanda.

Vanda.

atmosphere is essential. Frequent misting is also recommended – add a liquid feed to the sprayer. Because *Vanda* produce many aerial roots, they should be placed in a basket containing a very open compost; this serves only to anchor the plant. In practice, *Vanda* do not really need any compost at all and so the plant may be secured by tying it to a cane which has been wired on to the basket. As the plant ages, it will lose the lower leaves and eventually there will be a bare stem in the lower section. This section may be cut off and the plant secured into its basket.

All *Vanda* need plenty of light; those with terete leaves require almost full sun. The plants that really need hot, steamy conditions may be housed in a large cabinet that could be constructed within the greenhouse or in the home. If you install heating and a nebulizer, you will create the right conditions. In the home you may need to put in additional lighting.

Vanda.

BELOW LEFT: Vanda.

BELOW: Vanda.

Vanda.

BELOW: Vanda.

ZYGOPETALUM HOOKER

Sir William Hooker described this genus in 1827; the name derives from the Greek *zygon*, yoke and *petalon*, petal, referring to the yoke-like callus at the base of the labellum. There are about twenty species within the genus which is distributed through Central and South America to southern Brazil. *Zygopetalum* is a sympodial epiphytic or terrestrial plant.

General Description

The pseudobulbs of this plant are short, stout and generally ovoid; they tend to wrinkle with age and are topped by two or more leaves. The leaves are apical, glossy, distichous and plicate. The inflorescence emerges from the base of the new bulb and forms a raceme of few to many showy, highly scented flowers.

Culture

Zygopetalum (zye-go-pet-are-lum) are plants for the intermediate house (12–15°C/53–59°F). They like good light conditions, with light shade. Full sun is harmful to them. During active growth plenty of water and feed may be supplied. Be very careful when the new growths are developing since excessive humidity and water retention within the leaves will cause rotting. Also, on no account should the leaves be sprayed, as this will mark them.

The terrestrial *Zygopetalums* should be potted in a mixture of either peat, horticultural sand, vermiculite and fine-grade bark in a ratio of 2:2:1:1, or bark, moss and broken pieces of polystyrene in a ratio of 2:1:1, with the addition of dolomitic lime at 3g/ltr. The epiphytic species do well in compost similar to that for cattleyas. Propagation can be done by division at repotting time. Do not divide as a matter of course, but develop specimen plants that will produce many flower spikes.

The remaining plants to be described in this chapter are hardy terrestrial species.

BLETILLA RCHB. F.

The generic name is a diminutive of *Bletia*, an American terrestrial orchid whose flowers it resembles. *Bletilla* is a terrestrial genus of ten species, from eastern Asia, Taiwan and other nearby islands. The commonest species grown is *B. striata*; this is a plant available in many garden centres. The flowers are white or pink and flower in early summer.

General Description

It is deciduous and the stems form a corm-like pseudobulb from the short rhizome. The leaves are usually four in number; they are linear to obovate-lanceolate, plicate.

Culture

This is a hardy orchid. New plants should be planted in the garden in spring, with the corm just buried in friable soil enriched with leaf mould that is not likely to become waterlogged. It prefers light shade, in association with hardy ferns, but will also tolerate full sun. It is ideally suited to a woodland-edge garden, with acid conditions.

Zygopetalum.

PLEIONE DAVID DON

Its common name is Indian crocus. The genus was described by David Don, an English botanist, in 1825. The name comes from Greek mythology: Pleione, the mother of the Pleiades (the seven daughters of Atlas) who were transformed into a cluster of stars by Zeus. The genus has some sixteen species of epiphytic, lithophytic and terrestrial plants which are distributed throughout China, Taiwan, Tibet, Thailand and Burma. It is usually found growing on mossy rocks and trees at between 600 and 4,200m (2,000–14,000ft). These areas have winters that are generally dry and cold and during this time the plants survive in a dormant state as leafless pseudobulbs without any live roots. The genus is well known to alpine enthusiasts because *Pleione* grows well under the conditions of the alpine house.

General Description

It is a dwarf plant, growing into clusters. The stem is modified into a bulbous pseudobulb with a single deciduous, apical leaf. The flower is quite large in relation to the size of the plant. The lip is trumpet-shaped, trilobed and frilled or incised. Notable species are: *P. formosana* (*see* below), *P. forrestii*, *P. hookeriana*, *P. humilis*, *P. limprichtii*, *P. maculata*, *P. praecox* and *P. yunnanensis*. *The Genus Pleione*, by Cribb, is recommended reading for this genus. It also has a dedicated website: www. pleione.info

Culture

Pleione has always been considered to be a plant that has short-lived flowers; this is true and many flowers will last only two or three weeks. However, there are a couple of remedies to this problem. One is to select those species that flower at different times. By doing this you can extend the flowering period from October to May. Another is to have in your collection the hybrid forms which generally last longer than the species, outlasting them by a couple of weeks. They are best potted in shallow pans (half pots) containing a bark-based medium that has been enriched with leaf mould and moss. The compost could be two parts by volume of medium orchid bark and one of leaf mould–moss. They may be grown outdoors, in a cold greenhouse or the alpine house. They are probably better off outside where they can be cooler and receive all the summer rain. In the greenhouse they will need shading, good ventilation and plenty of air movement. For *Pleione*s

Pleione.

Pleione.

BELOW: Pleione.

the alpine type of greenhouse is ideal because it has windows opening the full length of the house on both sides and in the roof. Outdoors in the winter they will need to be protected, not so much from cold but from excessive wet weather. In order to keep them absolutely dry in winter cover them with a cloche; they should then succeed. *Pleione* should be given a high nitrogen feed early in the growing season, changing to a high potassium one later in the summer. As with many orchids, they are weak feeders and so dilute to half the recommended dosage.

Beginning in autumn, the leaves will brown; at this time watering should be eased off. By the time the leaves have dropped, watering should have ceased. If the plants are in pots outside they should be brought into a cold greenhouse to overwinter in a dry state. In late winter, during their dormancy period when the compost is quite dry but before the new growth is too far developed, they should be repotted. The bulbs can be simply pushed slightly into the compost with about one-third sticking out. Surround them with moss. Begin to water gradually as the new growth appears to promote flowering and leaf development, and increase the watering as the roots extend. It is probably a good idea to begin watering from the bottom as this will force the roots down. During active growth they will need copious amounts of water in order to build up large bulbs. Apply feed at fortnightly intervals, using a balanced feed. The plants may be returned to their outdoor site in late spring. *P. formosana* is an ideal candidate for outdoor culture; place several bulbs in a single pan since this will give you a better effect when they are in flower.

PTEROSTYLIS R. BROWN

Its common name is greenhood. *Pterostylis* is a genus of some sixty species of orchid, with a subterranean tuber and fibrous roots. The leaves form a basal rosette or may be reduced to bracts on the stem. The flowers are green with strips of, or tinted with, purple. The name derives from the Greek *pteron*, wing and *stylos*, meaning column or style, thus referring to the wings on the upper column. *Pterostylis* is an Australian species but also found in Papua New Guinea, New Caledonia and New Zealand.

Culture

These are ideal for the alpine or cold greenhouse. The leaves die down during the summer when they can have a dry rest. Begin to water gradually as the new growth is seen. They seem to respond well to watering from the bottom. Stand the pot on a tray of grit and keep this wet; the roots will travel downwards in search of water. The flowers appear from late winter to early spring. These are attractive little plants that will bulk up very quickly.

SERAPIAS LINDL.

This has the common name of tongue orchid. This genus is a Mediterranean plant with about ten species. The name derives from the Greek *selene*, meaning moon and *pedilon*, meaning slipper, referring to the crescent-shaped rim of the lip.

Culture

As with all terrestrial orchids, you will need a soil-based compost, but it should be well drained. The drainage can be improved with the addition of horticultural grit. Make up the growing medium from equal parts of compost and grit. Some species grow in limestone areas, and so you may find it beneficial to add dolomitic limestone or something similar to raise the pH. The plants will need to be in stable conditions, so the use of large pots is beneficial in these cases. Plant the tubers 25–75cm (1–3in) below the surface, but just cover the tuber with the compost and make up the rest with grit to prevent the rotting of the collar during growth.

Repot during the rest period in late summer. No water should be given during this time; begin to water only when the new shoots can be seen above the surface and a rosette is forming. It is a good idea to water from the bottom, again because of the danger of rotting. Carefully water during winter, keeping the compost just moist and avoid splashing the leaves. A winter minimum temperature of 1°C (34°F) is fine. Also give them as much light as possible, especially in northern European latitudes and similar areas. Cease to water as the leaves fade, sometime around May.

CHAPTER 16

Showing Your Orchids

When you get into orchid growing and maybe join a society you will almost certainly want to show your plants. To do this and win an award is a great incentive, and it is also recognition of your cultural achievements.

The judges of orchids take into consideration two things: the culture and the flower. If you intend to put anything up for judging you obviously need to present it at its best. Do not, therefore, have plants ravaged by insects with holes in the leaves and flowers. Go over the plant before you leave for the show and make sure that everything is in good condition. Listed below are a few pointers:

- Is the plant growing well, is it healthy and free from pests and disease?
- Are there are any dead or dying leaves? Cut these off as close to the plant as possible, or cut off the offending part of the leaf to a point; this is acceptable for any long, strap-like leaves.
- Likewise, you should not present a plant with too many old, leafless pseudobulbs; it indicates poor culture and that the plant is not repotted often enough.
- Ensure that the flower spikes are staked and neatly tied to a green-coloured split cane; you may use plastic-coated twist-tie wire; this is easy to handle and the ends can be cut close to the twisted part, thus leaving a neat tie.
- Stake the flower spikes as they grow; tie them loosely at first, making them more secure as they extend; if you attempt to tie the spike on to a

Cattleyas on the show bench.

cane later you run the risk of snapping the spike and the flowers may be oriented upside down.

- Ensure that the compost surface is clean and free from intruders such as ferns; many judges will mark you down or will not judge at all if there are other plants growing in the pot (poor culture).
- Likewise ensure that the outside of the pot is free from from moss and algae.
- Be very careful when you transport your plants to the show to prevent the risk of their breaking; pack around the pot with newspaper in a suitable carrying box; if you have a particularly delicate flower you should wrap this in tissue paper to transport it; make sure that the flower spikes are secure and that the pots or box will not move if you take a corner sharply or brake suddenly; take care and your plants will arrive in one piece.
- If you enter a class in which you display a group of orchids, make sure that the pots are well hidden or have all your plants in black pots, the reason being that judges consider that the pots are a distraction from the plants and therefore unsightly. There are many ways in which to hide pots: use black cloth, bury them in compost or collect leaves in the autumn and use these to pack around the pots. Speak to the judges and ascertain what the rules are and what they look for – take a good look at the first-prize winner's entry and make notes.

The judging panel will take their time inspecting all the details of the plants on show and will award points, or deduct points from 100. They will decide whether to award prizes or not, which is usually on a unanimous decision. In my society (The North of England Orchid Society) plants are judged for culture and merit. For each of these categories, half of the marks are available to give a total of 100. As you can see from the illustration opposite, judging is a matter of the careful assessment of the plant. The judges are considering how you have grown it and how well it has flowered. Presentation is only 5 per cent, but it could be a vital 5 per cent and give you a place. Since the two categories, merit and culture, are equally important, assessing the plant in more detail makes it possible to distinguish between them if there are two or more equally worthy. You can have any plant, thought worthy, judged for a higher award. A panel will consider those presented and give points under the following categories:

colour and texture:	10
shape + balance + carriage + overlap, where appropriate:	20
length of stem or spike + spacing (including spike habit):	10
aesthetic appeal:	15
size of flower:	10
number of flowers per lead or bulbs + allowance for the number of leads (ignore for *Paphiopedilums*):	15
substance:	10
progressive improvement:	5
rarity and difficulty of cultivation:	5
TOTAL:	**100** (*Paphiopedilums*: **85**)

When the points are calculated (as percentages) one of the following may be awarded:

FIRST-CLASS DIPLOMA	90 or more
DIPLOMA OF MERIT	84–89.9
VERY HIGHLY COMMENDED	80–83.9
HIGHLY COMMENDED	77–79.9
COMMENDED	74–76.9

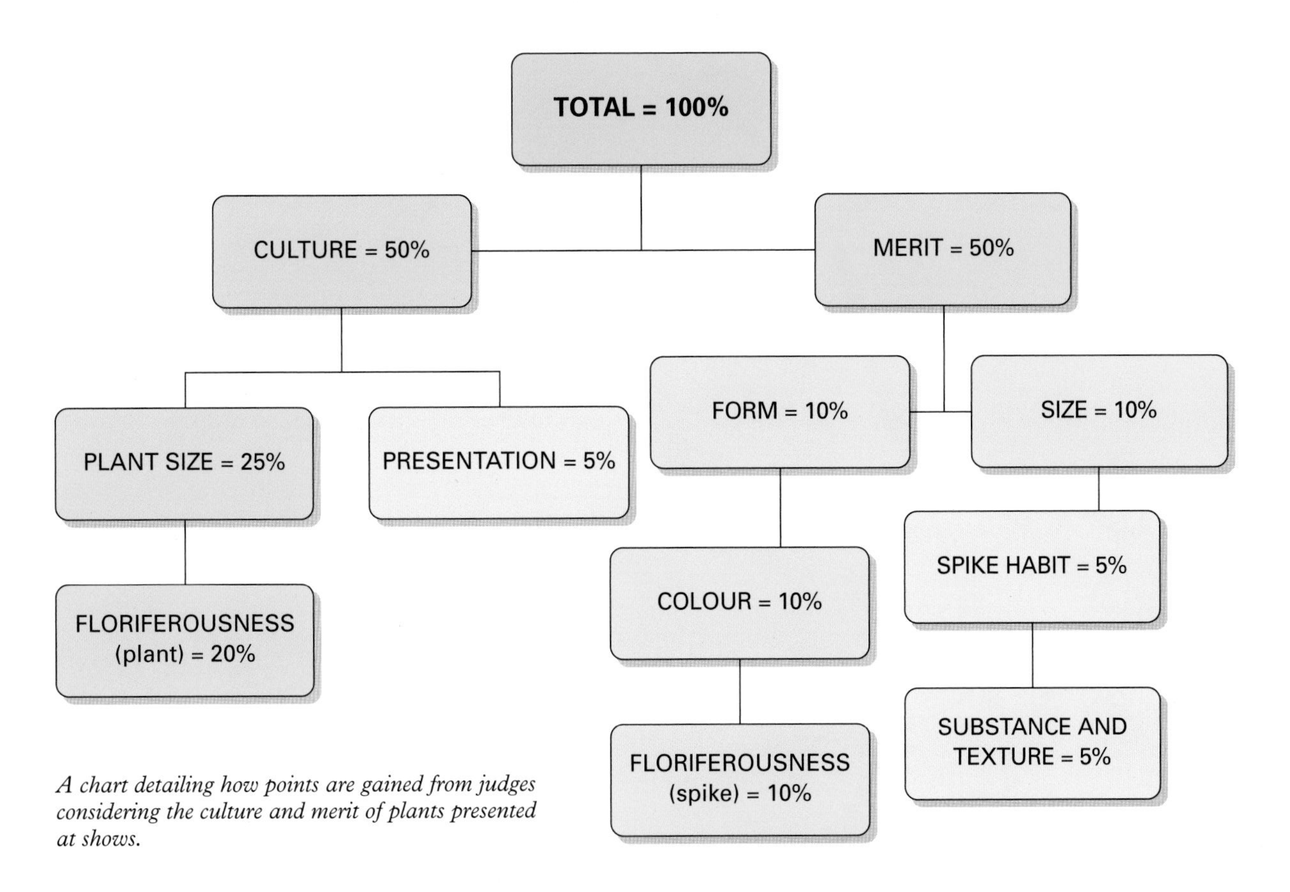

A chart detailing how points are gained from judges considering the culture and merit of plants presented at shows.

Encyclia radicans.

CHAPTER 17

Buying Orchids

Where to buy orchids and what to look for in a good plant are sometimes difficult decisions for the beginner. Orchids are available today in many places, from the specialist nursery, the garden centre, the DIY store or the local florist. They have become widely available and the price of them has become reasonable because of modern techniques in propagation. Those places other than the specialist nursery will have many unnamed hybrids of different genera on their shelves that are suitable for the home. If you want to see a wide range of named hybrids or species of a particular genus then you will have to visit the specialist nursery. Orchid nurseries may be found in all countries around the world. They may be general and offer orchids of many different genera, or they may specialize in a particular genus. Most orchid nurseries will send plants by mail order.

WHAT WILL YOU HAVE TO PAY?

This really depends on whether it is a named or an unnamed hybrid, a species or a specimen plant. The plants on sale in the garden centre will be the unnamed hybrids of the popular genera of *Phalaenopsis*, *Cymbidium*, *Dendrobium* or *Oncidium*, for instance. The orchid nurseries will have these same genera, but they will have named hybrids too and they will also have many more genera besides. The orchid nurseries will also have a large selection of species.

The unnamed hybrids from the garden centre will be the cheaper to buy, followed by the named hybrids and then the species from the nursery. You will also have to pay more for a larger plant of flowering size. The small, one- or two-year-old plants that will need to be brought on for a further year or two are usually good value; you just need to care for them and wait. Obviously, as a plant increases in size so does the price. Many nurseries will have special offers from time to time and these are always worth looking out for. Get on to the nursery's mailing list, because bargains will be snapped up quickly.

SPECIES OR HYBRIDS?

This really depends on the cultural conditions you can provide. Species, being the natural plant, is more demanding of its conditions than a hybrid. If you cannot provide these conditions then it is more likely to suffer. Thus most species are more likely to be confined to the greenhouse where the correct conditions can be provided. The hybrid has been bred or crossed between two plants and has in many cases been bred for the house-plant market. In the plant world, hybrids are sought after for their colour or scent. However, not all species are so demanding and many of them will live quite happily indoors.

At the garden centre displays of orchid plants draw admirers. People buy them for their mass of colourful, exotic blooms. Those on sale in the shops usually have a long flower life (weeks or even several months, in some cases). In your home, when they are in flower, they are beautiful, but perhaps the bare plant has little to offer in the way of decoration. In these cases you may choose to hide them among other house plants or possibly move them outdoors.

Likewise, the more specialist orchids from nurseries may have a short flowering period, only three or four days of glory in the whole year, leaving them unsuitable as house plants. If you are buying for the home choose thoughtfully what you will purchase, with an idea of where you will put it when it is not in flower. On the plus side though, many of those orchids suitable as house plants have interesting mottled foliage, such as *Paphiopedilums* and *Phalaenopsis*; there is even a cymbidium that has variegated leaves. This can extend the pleasure one gets from house plants when they are not in flower.

WHAT TO LOOK FOR WHEN BUYING AN ORCHID

Have a good look at the plant and also look at the roots (if possible) and the compost and consider the following points: are the leaves in good condition? Are the pseudobulbs solid, and not wrinkled? Are the flowers bright and not fading? Is the compost just moist, is it soaking or is it bone dry, and is the plant steady in the pot? Is the plant damaged? We can consider these questions in more detail and illustrate what to look for in a good plant.

Cattleya.

Are the Plant's Leaves in Good Condition?

By good condition I mean that the leaves should be nice and green, unless the leaves are mottled, when the colour should be good. The leaf should feel solid and not squashy in any way. The leaves of *Phalaenopsis* should not show signs of wrinkling; there should be no damage, either physical or insect.

Are the Pseudobulbs Solid?

The pseudobulbs of orchids should be solid; this indicates a plant that has been well watered and fed and is the sign of a healthy plant. If the 'bulb' is soft to pressure between finger and thumb then it has perhaps been overwatered, the roots dead and no more water is being taken up.

Are the Bulbs Wrinkled?

This may be a sign of underwatering and that the plant is using up its reserves. The wrinkling may not be too serious a problem and by reintroducing regular watering subsequently the plant should be fine.

Are the Flowers in Good Condition?

If they are not, then the plant has been in the nursery or shop for some time and the flowering cycle is over; however, this is not a sign of poor health. You may be able to get a discount on that plant, but examine it, referring to the other questions on this list. You may get a good plant at a reduced price.

Is the Compost in Good Condition?

The compost and the health of the roots are important considerations. You may be able to knock the plant gently from its pot and look at the roots. If you see healthy, white roots in moist compost then all will be well and the plant will be worth buying. *Phalaenopsis* are generally sold in transparent pots nowadays because they photosynthesize through their roots and you can see the condition of them through the pot. If, on the other hand, the compost is soggy, the plant loose in the pot and there is no sign of healthy roots, then it has been overwatered and you are probably best advised to leave it where it is. If the compost is very wet it may have just been watered, so inspect the plant. If it is very dry and the plant looks rather sick, wilted and limp, then the chances are that it is sick so leave it. Plants with pseudobulbs are better adapted to withstand some adversity, and, if the pot is dry, by rewatering the plants should be satisfactory. Plants such as *Phalaenopsis* or *Paphiopedilum* do not have pseudobulbs and cannot withstand long, dry periods; therefore if the compost is very dry then these may not be such good buys.

Is there Damage to the Plant?

Physical damage is not always a problem. If it concerns only the leaves, these can be cut off. If the damage is to the bulb, then disease may also be present and I would leave it alone. Not that it should be a problem in a nursery or shop, but you should look out for pests or pest damage to be sure that you are buying a healthy plant.

GENERAL POINTS

You should always inspect any plant before you buy it, and always consider the points above. You may see plants on the discounted shelf, and these are always worth a look. The reason for their being there may simply be they have finished flowering and a garden centre cannot easily sell plants that are not in flower. Depending on the genus, even if the plant has been allowed to dry out you may be able to bring it back to health. Those with pseudobulbs will withstand a short drought, rather than being too wet. Those without pseudobulbs may not survive excessively dry periods, and you will not know how long the plants have been on the shelf. If the compost has shrunk away from the pot side then it has been dry for some time; the plant in such a pot would therefore be a bad buy.

Plants from unknown sources are sometimes a worry as you will not know in what conditions they have been kept. It is good practice to quarantine any new plant for a few weeks. This should allow time for any pest eggs to hatch and you can deal with them in isolation without the risk of infecting the whole greenhouse.

It is always wise to buy your orchids from reliable sources such as specialist orchid nurseries and from people who know how to look after them. I do not want to criticize garden centres, but they may not know how to look after orchids and their staff will water them as with all the other plants, resulting in overwatered orchids. Likewise garden centres in DIY stores do not always look after their plants properly (although many do), so inspect any orchid before you buy it. They may have come down in price over the years, but they are still not cheap. You want to get the best value for your money and, with a little time spent looking, you should come away with a good plant.

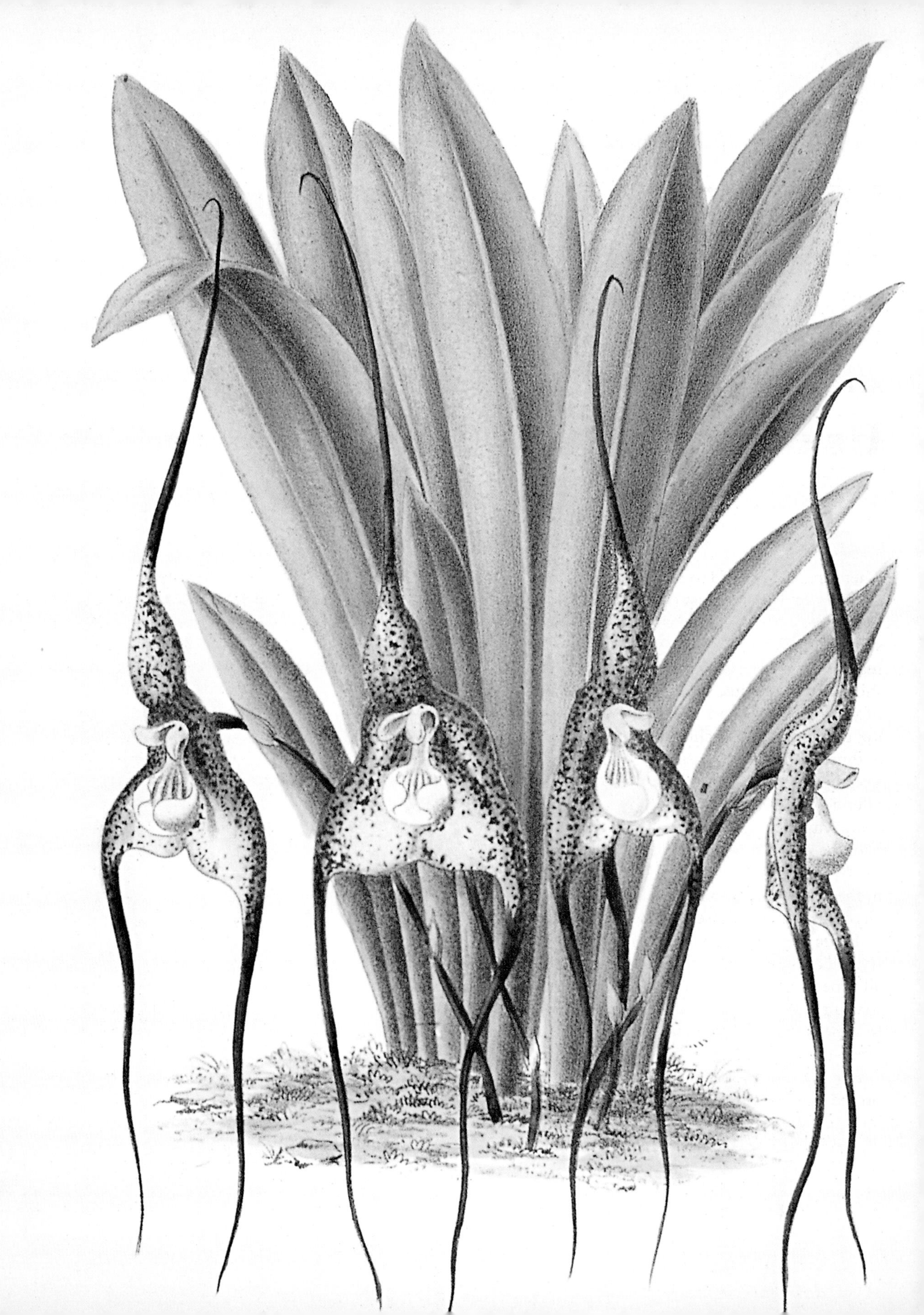

PART 4
APPENDICES

APPENDIX I

Useful Contacts and Addresses

There are many orchid societies and groups throughout the world. The format of their meetings will vary from society to society. They may have talks, demonstrations and shows, and they may partake in local, regional, national or even international orchid shows. In the United Kingdom there are currently fifty-two societies and all are dedicated to furthering the interests of orchid growing by the amateur enthusiast. Many are associated with the professional growers who set up stands to sell plants and offer advice at meetings and shows throughout the year. I have not listed any of the societies simply because names and addresses change. If you want to be put in contact with a society near you contact, in the United Kingdom, the British Orchid Council representative whose name is to be found below.

There are orchid nurseries throughout the country. All of these will gladly offer help and advice on all aspects of cultivation. Many offer special deals to beginners, with a selection of plants that are easy to cope with. They will also probably have special offers from time to time.

For details of your local society and the nearest orchid nursery in the United Kingdom check your local telephone directory or you may obtain a copy of *A Grower's Guide*. This useful booklet is published by the British Orchid Growers Association and the British Orchid Council. Copies may be obtained from the secretary of the BOC:

Mr E.S. Manning
'Estover'
25a Forest Road
Tarporley
Cheshire
CW6 0HX
telephone: 01829 732323
fax: 01829 732 355
email: boc@stevemanning.clara.co.uk

There are orchid societies and groups in most countries of the world – there may be a national society such as The American Orchid Society, for instance. I have not listed these societies either, but you can easily trace them through the Internet: typing 'orchid' in the search engine will produce thousands of links to societies, nurseries, photographs, cultural information, books and much more. Try searching by genus to limit the references that appear on the screen. One recommended site is the Hardy Orchid Society at www.HardyOrchid-Society.com.

APPENDIX II

Orchid Sundries Suppliers

Throughout this book I have described the equipment and materials associated with orchid growing. A company in England that specializes in orchid sundries for growers is:

Ratcliffe Orchids Ltd
Owslebury
Winchester
SO21 1LR
telephone: 01962 777 372
fax: 01962 777 664
email: ratcliffe@zoo.co.uk

Growth Technology Ltd is the supplier for liquid silicon and humic acid. Their web site is: www.growthtechnology.com

www.simplycontrol.com for general horticultural equipment; this company can supply a wide range of equipment enabling you to automate your greenhouse, such as humidity, lighting, heating, watering, insulation and shading and electronic control devices.

The Royal Botanic Gardens Kew, bookshop: telephone: 020 83 32 5000; web site: www.kew.org

The Royal Horticultural Society, Wisley, bookshop: telephone: 01483 211 113; web site: www.rhs.org.uk

Orchids by Post is a company that specializes in hardy orchids; web site: www.orchidsbypost.co.uk

The North of England Orchid Society (my own society) can be found at: Theneos@aol.com

Charles and Margaret Baker have produced a web page dealing with orchid culture: www.orchid-culture.com

A web page dealing with the vast subject of intergeneric orchid hybrids has been produced by Linda Fortner ('The Orchid Lady') in the USA; web site: www.orchidlady.com

Specific orchid culture; website: www.orchidculture.com

APPENDIX III

Humidity Chart

Use this chart to determine the relative humidity in your greenhouse:

1. take a reading from both the dry thermometer (T) and the wet thermometer (t);
2. calculate the degrees difference between the dry and the wet thermometer;
3. look down the left side of the chart (dry thermometer) and find that temperature reading;
4. move along to the right to the column beneath the difference; the number in the square is the relative humidity.

EXAMPLE: dry thermometer reading 16°C; wet reading 24°C; difference is 8°C; move across from 16 to beneath 8 and read 30 relative humidity: 30 per cent.

DIFFERENCE

Dry Bulb °C (T)	2.0	2.2	2.4	2.6	2.8	3.0	3.2	3.4	3.6	3.8	4.0	4.5	5.0	5.5	6.0	6.5	7.0	7.5	8.0	8.5
2	68	65	62	59	55	52	49	46	43	40	37	29	22	14	7	–	–	–	–	–
3	70	67	64	61	58	55	52	49	46	43	40	33	26	19	12	5	–	–	–	–
4	71	68	65	62	60	57	54	51	48	46	43	36	29	22	16	9	–	–	–	–
5	72	69	67	64	61	58	56	53	51	48	45	39	33	26	20	13	7	–	–	–
6	73	70	68	65	63	60	58	55	53	50	48	41	35	29	24	17	11	5	–	–
7	74	72	69	67	64	62	59	57	54	52	50	44	38	32	26	21	15	10	–	–
8	75	73	70	68	65	63	61	59	56	54	51	46	40	35	29	24	19	14	8	–
9	76	74	71	69	67	64	62	60	58	55	53	48	42	37	32	27	22	17	12	7
10	77	74	72	70	68	66	63	61	59	57	55	50	44	39	34	29	24	20	15	10
11	78	75	73	71	69	67	65	62	60	58	56	51	46	41	36	32	27	22	18	13
12	78	76	74	72	70	68	66	64	62	60	58	53	48	43	39	34	29	25	21	16
13	79	77	75	73	71	69	97	65	63	61	59	54	50	45	41	36	32	28	23	19
14	79	78	76	74	72	70	68	66	64	62	60	56	51	47	42	38	34	30	26	22
15	80	78	76	74	73	71	69	67	65	63	61	57	53	48	44	40	36	32	27	24

Dry Bulb °C (T)	2.0	2.5	3.0	3.5	4.0	4.5	5.0	5.5	6.0	6.5	7.0	7.5	8.0	8.5	9.0	9.5	10.0	10.5	11.0	11.5
16	81	76	71	67	63	58	54	50	46	42	38	34	30	26	23	19	15	12	8	5
17	82	77	72	68	64	60	55	51	47	43	40	36	32	28	25	21	18	14	11	8
18	82	77	73	69	65	61	57	53	49	45	41	38	34	30	27	23	20	17	14	10
19	83	78	74	70	65	62	58	54	50	46	43	39	36	32	29	26	22	19	16	13
20	83	78	74	70	66	63	59	55	51	48	44	41	37	34	31	28	24	21	18	15
21	83	79	75	71	67	64	60	56	52	49	46	42	39	36	32	29	26	23	20	17
22	83	80	76	72	68	64	61	57	54	50	47	44	40	37	34	31	28	25	22	19
23	84	80	76	72	69	65	62	58	55	52	48	45	42	39	36	33	30	27	24	21
24	84	80	77	73	69	66	62	59	56	53	49	46	43	40	37	34	31	29	26	23
25	84	81	77	74	70	67	63	60	57	54	50	47	44	41	39	36	33	30	28	25
26	85	81	78	74	71	67	64	61	58	54	51	49	46	43	40	37	34	32	29	26
27	85	82	78	75	71	68	65	62	58	56	52	50	47	44	41	38	36	33	31	28
28	85	82	78	75	72	69	65	62	59	56	53	51	48	45	42	40	37	34	32	29
29	86	82	79	76	72	69	66	63	60	57	54	52	49	46	43	41	38	36	33	31
30	86	83	79	76	73	70	67	64	61	58	55	52	50	47	44	42	39	37	35	32
31	86	83	80	77	73	70	67	64	61	59	56	53	51	48	45	43	40	38	36	33
32	86	83	80	77	74	71	68	65	62	60	57	54	51	49	46	44	41	39	37	35

APPENDIX IV

The pH Scale

The pH value is a measure of the hydrogen ion concentration in an aqueous solution; the formula for it is: $\log_{10}[1/(H^+)]$. The formula produces a value in which the higher the number of H^+ ions the lower the pH reading. The scale runs from 1.0 to 14.0, 1.0 being highly acid and 14.0 being highly alkaline, with 7.0 being neutral. The scale is logarithmic, so each unit change in it means a ten-fold change in the number of ions. To measure pH you can either use special papers that change colour and check these against a colour indicator chart, or by electrical means with the aid of a meter.

Most epiphytic orchids like slightly acidic conditions, but those that grow lithophytically on limestone will require more alkaline conditions. Terrestrial species from chalk grassland will be alkaline lovers and those from marshes and bogs will need acidic conditions.

APPENDIX V

Temperature Requirements for Various Genera

This list is by no means definitive but it has some of the better known plants. You will notice that some are in more than one column and so they will grow within that temperature range, that is, cool to intermediate (C–I) or intermediate to warm (I–W). The temperatures quoted are the winter minima.

Hardy growers ***4°C/39°F***	***Cool growers*** ***10°C/50°F***	***Intermediate growers*** ***15°C/59°F***	***Warm growers*** ***18°C/64°F***
Anacamptis sp.	*Anguloa clowesii*	*Aerides* sp.	*Angraecum*
Bletilla	*Angulocaste*	*Ansellia* sp.	*Calanthe*
Cephalanthera	*Bifrenaria*	*Ascocentrum* sp. (I–W)	*Coelogyne asperata*
Cypripedium	*Brassia*	*Bletia*	*C. pandurata*
Dactylorhiza	*Chysis* sp. (C–W)	*Brassolaeliacattleya*	*Doritis pulcherrima*
Epipactis	*Cattleya aurantiaca*	*Brassovola*	*Oncidium papilio*
Goodyera	*Coelogyne cristata*	*Bulbophyllum* (all ranges)	*Paphiopedilum bellatulum*
Gymnadenia (fragrant)	*Coelogyne ochracea*	*Catasetum*	*Phalaenopsis* sp. and hybrids
Hammarbya (bog orchid)	*Cymbidium*	*Cattleya bowringiana*	*Vanda* sp. (I–W)
Herminium (musk orchid)	*Dendrobium aureum*	*Dendrobium transparens*	
Himantoglossum (lizard orchid)	*D. densiflorum*	*D. pieradii*	
Liparis	*D. nobile*	*Eria coronaria*	
Listera	*Dracula* sp.	*Gongora galeata*	
Neottia	*Encyclia citrina*	*Huntleya burtii*	
Ophrys (bee orchid)	*Encyclia cochleata*	*L. virginalis* (C–I)	
Orchis (military orchid)	*Epidendrum ibaguense*	*Laelia purpurata*	
Platanthera (butterfly orchid)	*Gomesa crispa*	*Lycaste aromatica* (C–I)	
Pseudorchis	*Laelia anceps*	*Miltonia* sp.	
Serapias (tongue orchid)	*Masdevallia* sp.	*Oncidium* sp. and hybrids (C–I)	
Spiranthes (autumn, ladies' tresses)	*Maxillaria tenuifolia*	*Paphiopedilum callosum*	
	M. picta	*Promenaea* sp.	
	Odontioda	*Rhychostylis*	
	Odontoglossum sp. and hybrids	*Sobralia macrantha* (C–I)	
	Paphiopedilum insigne (hybrids)	*Sophronitis coccinea* (C–I)	
		Stanhopea (C–I)	
		Thunia sp. (C–I)	
		Vuylstekeara ('Cambria Plush')	
		Zygopetalum sp.	

Glossary

aerial (aerial roots) Root borne wholly above ground, either adventitiously from the stem or the basal rooting axis as in many epiphytes.
adventitious (adventive) Occurring in an unusual location, originally from other than the normal place, applied to buds developing along a stem rather than at leaf axils; to viviparously-produced plantlets and to roots that develop not from the radical and its subdivisions but from another part such as the stem or the leaf axil.
aerial root Root of an epiphytic orchid which has a soft outer layer of cells that are capable of absorbing and holding considerable amounts of water; there is a central core that transfers the water and nutrients to the plant; these roots also provide support for the plant.
alliance A group of related genera. The term often relates direct to the more botanical sub-tribe; thus the pleurothallid alliance consists of those genera in the sub-tribe Pleurothallidinae. Less formally but more significantly, the ondontoglossum alliance contains the genus *Ondontoglossum* and its near relations (allies).
angular (angulate) With laterally projecting angles, as in longitudinally ridged and angled stems.
anther The pollen-bearing portion of the stamen, either sessile or attached to a filament.
anther cap The case enclosing the pollinia.
apex The growing point of a stem or root; the tip of an organ or structure, most commonly used of a leaf.
apical Borne at the apex of an organ, farthest from the point of attachment; pertaining to the apex.
appressed (adpressed) Of indumentum (hairs), leaves, leaf sheath, for instance; used of an organ which lies flat and close to the stem or leaf to which it is attached.
autogamous Self-fertilizing.
axil The upper angle between an axil of any axis and any offshoot or lateral organ arising from it, especially a leaf.
bract A modified, protective leaf associated with the inflorescence (clothing the stalk and subtending the flowers), with buds and newly emerging shoots and stems.
coriaceous Leathery or tough but smooth and pliable in texture.
corymb An indeterminate, flat-topped or convex inflorescence, where the outer flowers open first; cf. umbel.
dicotyledon One of the two great divisions of angiosperms (flowering plants) in which the embryo characteristically has two cotyledons (seed leaves), sometime more.
distichous Of leaves – being arranged in two opposite ranks along a stem or branch. As in *Angraecum distichum* or *Phalaenopsis* leaves.
epiphyte A plant that uses another, usually a tree, for support and to gain height in a rainforest where on the forest floor light levels are too low.
equitant When conduplicate leaves overlap or stand inside each other in two ranks in a strongly compressed fan.
flaccid Weak, limp, floppy or lax; sometimes lacking fluids within cells.
FYM Farm yard manure; use only well-rotted material. It is usually mixed with bark or other products to provide a medium for terrestrial species.
keiki A plantlet developing adventitiously on a cane-like stem, a pseudobulb, inflorescence branch or, very rarely, on a root.
labellum (lip) The enlarged or otherwise distinctive third petal of an orchid, developing as a landing platform for pollinators.

lanceolate Lance-shaped, narrowly ovate, but 3–6 times as long as broad and with the broadest point below the middle, tapering to a spear-like apex.
lax Loose (e.g. flowers) in an inflorescence or loose arrangement of leaves.
Linnaeus Carl von Linné, Swedish botanist known as the father of modern taxonomy.
monocotyledon (**monocot**) The monocots are one of the two primary divisions of the angiosperms (flowering plants), the other being dicots. They are characterized by a single, not double, cotyledon in the seed. They usually lack cambium and thus woody tissue and in many cases have parallel venation. The monocotyledons include Gramineae, Musaceae, Agavaceae, Lilliaceae, Amaryllidaceae, Orchidaceae, Araceae, Iridaceae, Bromeliaceae and Palmae.
monopodial growth Growth is vertical with the new leaf emerging from the centre of the plant. *Phalaenopsis* and *Vanda* are typical of this form.
mycorrhiza Literally 'fungus-root'; an association of fungal mycellium.
mycorrhizal Term describing roots which associate with a fungal mycelium and can derive a benefit through symbiosis or digestion from the latter.
node The point on an axis where one or more leaves, shoots, whorls, branches or flowers are attached.
panicle An indeterminate branched inflorescence, the branches generally racemose or corymbose.
pedicel The stalk supporting an individual flower or fruit; in Orchidaceae this is often replaced by a stalk-like ovary.
peduncle The stalk of an inflorescence.
perianth The collective term for the floral envelopes, the corolla and calyx, especially when the two are not clearly differentiated.
petal One of the modified leaves of the corolla, generally brightly coloured and often providing a place on which pollinators can alight.
petaloid Petal-like in colour, shape and texture.
petiole The leaf stalk.
petiolate Furnished with a petiole.
photosynthesis The series of metabolic reactions in plants, whereby organic compounds are synthesized by the reduction of carbon dioxide by energy absorbed by chlorophyll from sunlight.
plantlet A small or secondary plant developing on a larger one.
plicate Folded lengthwise, pleated, as a closed fan.
pollinium A regular mass of more or less coherent pollen grains.
polystichous Arranged in many rows.
pseudobulb (false bulb) The water-storing, thickened bulb-like stems found in many sympodial orchids – predominately aerial species and a feature of epiphytic or lithophytic species, but also in some terrestrials (e.g. *Eulophia* and *Calanthe*), where they may be buried. Pseudobulbs arise from a rhizome, sometimes so short as to give the appearance of being clumped. They vary in shape and size from species to species and usually grow actively for only one season, persisting thereafter as back-bulbs.
pseudocopulation A strategy whereby orchid flowers mimic the females of the pollinator species, attracting the males of that species whose frantic but vain sexual activity effects pollination. A ruse best illustrated by *Ophrys* and *Arthrochilus*.
pubescent Generally hairy; more specifically, covered with short, fine, soft hairs.
raceme An indeterminate, unbranched and usually elongate inflorescence composed of pedicelled flowers. The inflorescences of most orchids are strictly spicate, the individual flower 'stalks' being ovaries; however, this term tends to be confined to plants with compact, slender inflorescences (e.g. *Arpophyllum*), whereas the looser flower sprays, of *Cymbidium* for example, are described as racemes or said to be racemose. To confuse matters, growers habitually refer to most multiflowered orchid inflorescences as 'spikes'.
racemose Of flowers borne of a raceme; of an inflorescence that is a raceme.
raft A plaque made of wooden slats, cork bark pieces, used as a foothold for epiphytic orchids.
rhizome A modified stem, which bears roots and leaves and usually persists from season to season. In the case of orchids the rhizome is above ground and has modified stems or pseudobulbs.
saprophyte/saprophytic A plant deriving nutrition from dead or dying organic matter and usually lacking chlorophyll. Several orchids are saprophytic, including the coral root, the ghost orchid, bird's nest orchid, the giant climbing *Galeola* and the subterranean *Rhizanthella*. Because of their highly specialized habitats and fragile symbiotic association, they rarely survive in cultivation.

sessile Stalkless.

sheath A tubular structure surrounding an organ or part; most often the basal part of a leaf surrounding the stem, either inrolled as a tube, or strongly conduplicate and therefore distinct from the leaf blade.

sheathing Where the tubular, convolute or conduplicate base of a leaf or spathe invests and surrounds the stem or other parts.

spike An indeterminate inflorescence bearing sessile flowers on an unbranched axis; *see also* raceme.

stamen The male floral organ, bearing an anther, generally on a filament, and producing pollen.

stigma/stigmatic The apical unit of a pistil which receives the pollen and normally differs in texture from the rest of the style; relating to the stigma.

style The elongated and narrow part of the pistil between the ovary and the stigma; absent if the stigma is sessile.

sympodial The form of growth in which the terminal bud dies or terminates in an inflorescence and growth is continued by successive axes growing from lateral buds; cf. monopodial.

sympodial growth The growth habit is generally horizontal, but may be climbing. The plant produces a pseudobulb at intervals along a rhizome. The pseudobulb interval may be short giving the appearance of a clump of several centimetres.

terminal At the tip or apex of a stem; the summit of an axil.

terrestrial A plant that survives with its root system entirely in the ground.

throat The orifice of the tubular part of the lip.

tomentose With densely woolly, short, rigid hairs, perceptible to the touch.

terete Cylindrical and smoothly circular in cross-section, as in the leaves of *Lusidia* and *Papilionanthe* and some species of *Vanda* and *Dendrobium*.

trifoliate Three-leaved.

tuber/tubiferous A swollen, generally subterranean stem, branch or root used for storage; cf. tuberoid: bearing tubers.

turgid More or less swollen or inflated, sometimes by fluid contents.

unifoliate Bearing a single leaf.

vaginate Possessing or enclosed by a sheath.

variegated Marked irregularly with various colours.

velamen Corky epidermis of aerial roots in some epiphytes, through which atmospheric moisture is absorbed.

whorl When three or more organs are arranged in a circle at one node or near one another around the same axis.

Bibliography

Bechtel, H., P. Cribb and E. Launert, *The Manual of Cultivated Orchid Species* (London: Blandford, 1981)

Cribb, P., *The Genus Pleione* (Portland: Timber Press, 1988)

Hodgson, M., R. Paine and N. Anderson, *Orchids of the World* (London: Letts, 1991)

La Croix, I. and E., *African Orchids in the Wild and in Cultivation* (Portland, OR: Timber Press, 1997)

Leroy-Terquem, G. and J. Parisot, *Orchids, Care and Cultivation* (London: Cassell, 1991)

Rittershausen, B. and W., *Orchids as Indoor Plants* (London: Blandford, 1980)

Rittershausen, B. and W., *Orchid Growing Illustrated* (London: Blandford, 1985)

Schelpe, S. and J. Stewart, *Dendrobiums – an Introduction to the Species in Cultivation* (Dorset: Orchid Sundries, 1990)

Stewart, J., *Orchids at Kew* (London: HMSO, 1992)

Stewart, J. and M. Griffiths, *Manual of Orchids* (London: Macmillan, 1992)

Thompson, P.A., *Orchids from Seed* (London: Royal Botanic Gardens, Kew)

Williams, J.G., A.E. Williams and N. Arlott, *Orchids: a Field Guide to Britain and Europe* (London: Collins, 1978)

Index